LITTLE,
BROWN

1837

LARGE
PRINT

Against Medical Advice

A TRUE STORY

James Patterson

AND

Hal Friedman

LITTLE, BROWN AND COMPANY

LARGE PRINT

A list of other books by James Patterson is on page 349. For previews of upcoming books by James Patterson and more information about the author, visit www.JamesPatterson.com.

Little, Brown and Company
Hachette Book Group
237 Park Avenue, New York, NY 10017
Visit our Web site at www.HachetteBookGroupUSA.com

First Large Print Edition: October 2008
The Large Print Edition published in accord with the standards of the N.A.V.H.

Little, Brown and Company is a division of Hachette Book Group, Inc. The Little, Brown name and logo are trademarks of Hachette Book Group, Inc.

ISBN 978-0-316-02504-1
LCCN 2008924211

10 9 8 7 6 5 4 3 2 1

RRD-IN

Printed in the United States of America

To the Angels

To Dr. Ruth Bruun, the angel who pulled us up when our own wings were broken. Your dedication to all of your patients who have struggled with Tourette's syndrome cannot be measured, and you are loved and renowned for your profound wisdom and very great heart.

And to Jessie, our daughter, who weathered a childhood filled with great sadness and great inspiration. And yes, one day we will go to Disneyland.

—Hal and Sophia Friedman

Cory's Dedication

In my thirteen-year search for help, I traveled to places far from home and met many people, young and old, with medical conditions so extreme that I could not have imagined they existed.

I will never forget these special friends and their heroic battles with the phantoms that inhabited their minds.

I understand them, and they understand me.

I hope that this account of my life, which in many ways might be similar to theirs, will give them and others like them a measure of comfort and hope. And I'm grateful to my father and to James Patterson for helping to tell my story to the many people who might benefit from it.

To those like me, who are forced to travel a road that few others can even conceive of, I wish you peace, and a way home.

—Cory Friedman

Preface

"ONE MORNING in MARCH of 1989, just before my fifth birthday, I woke up as a normal, healthy boy. By that afternoon, I had an irresistible urge to shake my head — continually — and the course of my life changed in ways few people had ever seen or could begin to understand.

"Before long, my body became an explosive, volatile, and unpredictable force with a mind and personality of its own. It jerked and twisted, bent in half, and gyrated without warning until I was almost always in motion.

"I bit down on my teeth until I actually broke them and howled in pain because of the exposed nerves.

"I twisted my back around with such force that I tore muscle tissue and had to be drugged asleep to stop myself from doing it.

"My mind fed me thoughts so frightening I couldn't even talk about them to my parents.

"It didn't take long before I saw myself as the oddest person in my town. I felt like a boy on the end of a puppeteer's string.

"What made it even worse was knowing that I was also the puppeteer."

This is the story of Cory Friedman, and what follows is his remarkable journey, a story of triumph against all odds.

I met Hal Friedman in 1975 in New York City, at the J. Walter Thompson advertising agency, where we were both writers. We never imagined then that more than thirty years later, we would collaborate to write a book about Hal's son's heart-wrenching experiences.

Over the years, I would hear about Cory and his devastating struggle with Tourette's syndrome, obsessive-compulsive disorder, and anxiety disorder. But until Hal asked me to read an early draft he had written of Cory's story, I had no idea how severe a torment this lovely family had been living through. I knew that his complex condition was nearly impossible to treat. In fact, thirteen doctors and approximately sixty potent medicines after Cory's first traumatic head shakes, his debilitating symptoms were still unchecked.

When the downward spiral of his symptoms led to severe depression and hopelessness, and when all of Cory's doctors and their advice and medicines had proved to be false hopes, Cory's family staged an intervention that was as daring as anything that had preceded it, maybe even more so.

I was drawn to Cory's harrowing story because of what it says about the power of love, courage, and determination, and I was proud to join Hal in writing it. I knew that Cory's story had to be told because it would give hope and comfort to so many others struggling in all walks of life. Cory was in a living hell, but in climbing out, he showed us that it is possible to survive—and even thrive—against unbelievable odds. For me, that makes him a hero.

Hal and I are honored to bring you *Against Medical Advice* on Cory's behalf. My hope is that you, too, will be inspired by the courage, heartbreak, sacrifice, and ultimate victory of Cory Friedman and his family, and by the sheer invincibility of the human spirit.

—James Patterson

A Father's Prologue

THE EVENTS RECOUNTED HERE took place over what seemed like—to those of us who lived it—an endless thirteen-year period covering Cory's life from age five to age seventeen. We decided, with Cory's blessing, to tell his story in his own voice, because this conveys most powerfully what it was like for Cory to live through these experiences.

Some names and other identifying details of friends, doctors, and medical institutions have been changed.

The extremely unusual events portrayed in this story have been reconstructed from Cory's own accounts, from detailed medical diaries that were kept by his mother throughout the period, and from direct family observations. Cory confirms that this narrative presents an accurate portrait of his life story.

Over the four years it took to write this book, I was continuously tormented by the decision of whether or not to make the most intimate details of Cory's life public. Finally, I went to Cory for the guidance I needed, and he resolved the issue in a single sentence, without hesitation:

"If it will help other people like me, yes."

— *Hal Friedman*

Part One

A LOST CHILDHOOD

Chapter 1

I'M SEVENTEEN YEARS OLD and lying like a pathetic, helpless lump in the backseat of our family car, being transported to a place that treats crazy people.

This is an exceptional event, even for me. I know that my brain causes unusual problems that no one has been able to treat, but being insane isn't one of them.

How and why I've gotten to this point is complicated, but the main reason I'm here is more immediate. I've finally found the one thing that brings me peace—alcohol.

Now this self-medication has become a life-threatening danger that I cannot fix by myself. The doctors at the place I'm going to promise they can help me. I've heard that one before.

After about an hour, we arrive at a large brick building with a sign that reads DRESSLER PSYCHIAT-RIC HOSPITAL. In a split second the reality of what's happening becomes very real and very scary.

"Why does it say that?" I call from the backseat, my heart suddenly pounding.

"Don't worry about the sign," my mother says to calm my rising panic. "They treat all different kinds of problems here, Cory."

Dad looks as worried as I am but says softly, "Let's not deal with this now, okay?"

Not deal with going to a hospital for psychos? Sure, no problem. What can my father be thinking?

Inside the main entrance, I enter a very crowded, somewhat noisy waiting room. Being on view always makes me uneasy, so as soon as I start to walk, my feet need to perform a triple hop, three quick steps only inches apart, which throws me off balance.

I have to do this in order to satisfy a tension that is building up in my legs and can't be released any other way. Sometimes this trips me up so much that I go flying to the ground.

I do the triple hop a few more times before reaching out for the safety of one of the empty waiting-room chairs.

Welcome to my fun house, folks.

Chapter 2

MANY OF THE PEOPLE in the waiting area are still staring at me as my right hand shoots up in the air with the middle finger extended. *Oh boy, here we go,* I think. Giving people the bird is another one of my involuntary movements, or tics, that pop up exactly when they shouldn't. Try telling people that one's not deliberate.

Another middle-finger salute. *Hi, everybody!*

For a moment I think about the new medicines I'm taking, which are, as usual, not doing their job. Wellbutrin for depression, Tenex to keep me calm, Topamax as an "experiment" to see if a seizure medicine will help. So far I've been on fifty or sixty different medicines, none of which have worked—and a few of them can become deadly when washed down with Jack Daniel's.

Psychiatric hospital. A place for insane people, I'm thinking.

I know I'm not insane, even though the things I do make me look that way. But I do have a fear that I can think myself insane, and being in this place could push me over the edge. Going insane is probably my worst fear. If it happens, I won't know what, or *where,* reality is. To me, that's the ultimate isolation—to be separated from my own mind.

Eventually a receptionist calls my name and then starts asking me strange, bewildering questions. One of my eyes begins to twitch rapidly, and my tongue jumps out of my mouth like a snake's.

Occasionally I make a loud grunting sound like I've been punched hard in the stomach. Often my tics come one at a time, but today they're arriving in clusters of three or four, probably due to the stress.

I once told my parents that they couldn't live through a single day with what I go through *every day of my life,* and that was when I was a lot better than I am now.

It takes another hour or so for my parents to be interviewed by a doctor. When they come out, I can see that my mother has been crying. My father looks exhausted and edgy.

When it's my turn with the doctor, I can't stop myself from shooting him the bird, too. The guy is good about it. He totally ignores it. He's young and gentle and pretty much puts me at ease.

"I drink more than I should at night," I tell him, skipping the part about almost burning down my parents' house when I passed out on the couch with a lit cigarette. "I guess I like to get a little tipsy."

This is the understatement of the year. *Tipsy* is my code word for totally wasted.

The doctor gives me a complete physical, and when it's over he says I'm as healthy as anyone he's seen, which strikes me as very funny.

"So I guess I can go now?" I joke, punctuated by an involuntary tongue thrust.

"Yeah, right."

Later, back in the waiting area, a male attendant approaches us and asks for any medicines we might have brought.

"What do you mean?" my father asks.

"He needs these," my mother cautions, taking out a large plastic bag crammed with pill bottles.

"The doctors will take care of that," the attendant answers.

Mom reluctantly turns over the stash.

A while later, a female nurse approaches and leads the three of us deep into the rear of the building.

Everything is a lot different here. It's darker and there aren't any people around. It's a spooky place.

I fight off a really bad feeling that I'm going somewhere I won't be able to handle.

Eventually we stop in front of a massive door with a sign that says JUVENILE PSYCHIATRIC WARD D.

Mental kids, I think.

"That's not me," I snap, pointing to the sign. "Mom, you know I'm not crazy."

The nurse says, "We get all kinds of people here," as though arriving at an insane asylum is an ordinary event in anybody's life.

"You're here for your drinking," Mom adds, "which they treat."

"It doesn't say that on the signs."

The nurse takes a large metal key out of her jacket pocket, and I freeze at the sight of it. I've never been in a hospital where the doors have to be locked. I come to a sudden realization: You don't lock doors to keep people *out.* You lock doors to keep them *in.*

Chapter 3

DAD GETS IT, too. He and I exchange fearful glances, and he lightly touches my arm.

The door opens as if it weighs a thousand pounds. When I refuse to move, my father holds on to my arm tightly and guides me into the ward. The main corridor is small, maybe fifty feet long, before it turns off at a right angle. There are no nurses, doctors, or equipment around, not like any hospital I've been in.

Three boys are standing together at the end of the hall. They stare at me and whisper to one another. Then they disappear.

A man hunched over a computer in a small office

turns out to be the ward supervisor. He's dressed in very casual clothes and doesn't look like a doctor.

He keeps working for a while, and when he finally turns to us, I notice that his eyes are unfocused. He seems to be either stoned or a little retarded. If I didn't know who he was, I'd guess he was a patient.

After going over my papers, he leads the three of us farther into the ward. There are small offices on either side of the main corridor. One of them is for dispensing medicine and has metal bars over the opening.

We take a sharp right turn. All of the patients' rooms are off this corridor. There's also a common area with a TV playing, but no one is watching it.

"How many kids are here?" I ask.

"Right now, eleven. Never more than fifteen. That's a hospital rule."

As we pass by the rooms, I count about eight kids and have no idea where the rest are hiding. All are teenagers, none as old as I am.

The three boys I saw before appear again at the end of this corridor. As I get closer, they split up and walk past me, deadly serious. This is not a bunch I want to be around when the lights go out. And that includes the supervisor.

I'm getting more uncomfortable by the second. My skin is oozing a cold sweat. Hop. Hop. Hop.

I can't do this. I'm ticcing like crazy now.

In a moment we come to a large sign on the wall with rules printed in thick black letters.

NO TWO IN A ROOM
DOORS MUST REMAIN OPEN AT
ALL TIMES
ALL ARTICLES IN THE PATIENT'S
POSSESSION UPON ADMISSION WILL
BE CONFISCATED
PERMISSION REQUIRED TO LEAVE
PREMISES
AT ALL TIMES
NO STANDING ON WINDOWSILLS
NO STANDING ON UPPER BUNKS

I wonder about this last one, then look up at the ceiling and understand. The entire area is covered with a metal grating. The openings in the grid are too small to put your hand through. *This whole ward is a giant cage.*

My heart is pounding as if it wants to jump right out of my chest and die on the hospital floor. *How bad must this place be if people have tried getting out through the ceiling?*

"I'm not staying here!" I shout to my parents. "Don't you understand? I can't do this."

I back away, then turn and start for the main door, the only way out.

I want to run but hold myself in check so it doesn't look like I'm trying to escape; I don't want anyone to come chasing after me.

"I'm not like these people," I call back to my father.

My sudden decision throws my parents into confusion. I think coming to a place that looks like this is as much of a shock for them as it is for me.

"I'm not crazy! This place will *make* me crazy."

My father's expression changes slightly, and I can see in it a small ray of hope. He seems sympathetic yet angry at the same time, and I can't read which emotion is winning.

"You can't give up without trying," he says finally. "Give it time to work out."

"I'm *leaving*. Didn't you hear me?"

"What choice do you have? Think about it. This isn't your choice anymore."

This message sends me into a rage. I'm spinning out of control. I'll crash my way out if I have to.

I quickly rush to the door and stop when I see that there's another *golden rule* on it, etched on a bronze plate. This one stops me cold.

NO ONE PERMITTED OUTSIDE AFTER 6 P.M.

My watch says seven twenty. We've already been in this so-called hospital for more than three hours.

I try the door anyway. It doesn't move, not even a jiggle.

My anxiety spikes way past panic. If they lock me up, my life will be over. I'll die of fear. *People can die of fear. I've read about it.*

"Take a few deep breaths and try to calm down," my mother says when she catches up to me. "I know you're scared, Cory. We'll work something out. We always do."

"I promise I'll stop drinking on my own," I plead, my voice cracking. I'm completely helpless, dependent on her—as usual. "I swear it. Please, Mom, I know I can do it on my own. *Don't make me stay!*"

Chapter 4

WE'RE BACK in the supervisor's office, and he's just returned after leaving us alone for a few minutes to talk. My parents are having a really hard time deciding what to do. My father is usually fast with decisions, but this one is giving him trouble.

Finally, he takes a breath and delivers the words I've been praying for. "We don't think this is what we need for our son after all. We had a different idea of the hospital before we came."

I'm joyous inside. My father has done a complete about-face and is now going to fight for me. I want to hug him.

Unbelievably, the supervisor isn't taking my father seriously. He shakes his head as if he doesn't care what my dad just said.

"I'd appreciate you letting us out," my father announces.

He has to say it again before it seems to sink in with the guy.

"It's not possible for Cory to leave," the supervisor reports without any emotion. "Once a patient is admitted to the ward, New York State requires a minimum seventy-two-hour stay. It's the law."

"But we're *not* admitting him," my father explains. "We're going to leave right now, *before* he's admitted."

"He's already admitted," the man says more strongly. "It happened when he came through that door. Seventy-two hours, no exceptions," he adds, delivering what to him are just simple facts.

To me the number of hours — seventy-two — is like a death sentence to be executed in slow motion.

My father jumps up. "I want to speak to the hospital administrator," he barks. When the supervisor still doesn't react, he says, "Let me put it another way. I *demand* to speak to the administrator."

The supervisor thinks about it, then shrugs and picks up his phone. In a minute he hands the receiver to my dad.

My mother and I look at each other nervously. Everything is riding on this next conversation.

My father takes the phone and tells the administrator what's going on. He listens for a long time, and my mother and I don't know what's being said.

"There has to be a way," he says finally, obviously very frustrated. "What if someone came here by mistake, like we have?"

The debate continues, and he's beginning to lose his temper, which isn't like him.

"Even a criminal can post bond and get out of jail. What do you want me to do, call a lawyer?"

My father keeps going at the administrator. It seems hopeless. Then, all at once, he stops talking. "Yes, I understand. Thank you. I will." He hangs up and turns to us. "Maybe" is all he says.

Mom and I are both surprised when we hear who he's calling next.

"Dr. Meyerson! Thank God you picked up."

Dr. Meyerson is my current therapist. It's an absolute stroke of luck that he has answered his phone this late in the evening. We usually get his answering machine.

"We have an emergency here, and you're our only hope," my father continues.

The two of them talk for a few more minutes as he explains the situation.

After a while he lets out a deep breath.

"Say it just like that?" he asks. "Exactly that way?" He nods to us, then thanks Dr. Meyerson and hangs up.

My father turns to the supervisor and announces defiantly, "I request the release of my son *AMA*."

The man cocks his head suspiciously but doesn't respond. Not a word.

My father repeats the special code letters, this time as an order. "We are leaving the hospital with our son AMA. I'm told you understand what that means."

In a moment, the supervisor nods reluctantly, then gets on the phone again.

While he's talking to someone high up, my father explains, "*AMA* is an acronym for *against medical advice*. It's a legal code that allows the hospital to go around the law. It means that we understand the hospital advises against it, and it shifts responsibility to us—the parents—and our therapist. It lets the hospital off the hook in case a patient...harms himself or something."

"You know I wouldn't do that," I reply, to reinforce his decision.

"It's the only way we have a chance of getting you out of here."

"And what if we'd never learned about AMA?" my

18

mother asks. "Or if Dr. Meyerson wasn't around or didn't pick up?"

My father shakes his head. "We were lucky. Very lucky."

I study my father's face. He looks older than I've ever seen him. He's worn out. It's been as long a day for him as for me.

"Sorry, Dad."

He nods, but he isn't happy. "You know that we haven't fixed what we came here for."

It's not a question.

A long time later, the nightmare is finally ending. The supervisor is still waiting for whatever approvals he needs. My breathing has almost returned to normal.

Eventually someone comes into the ward with papers and the required signatures. The supervisor gets his key, and the thousand-pound door swings open again.

It's been five hours since we entered the hospital. I walk out the front door without looking back.

The ride home to New Jersey is silent. No one has the energy to say anything, and nothing we can talk about seems important compared to what's just happened.

My mother lets me smoke a cigarette, then a second one, and after that I fall asleep. In an hour or so, they wake me in New Jersey and I drag myself into our darkened house.

"I really mean it, Mom. I'm going to quit drinking," I tell her before going to bed. "I know I can do it."

I'm not lying. I really believe I can.

It's the middle of the week, and my resolve lasts until Friday night, when my body is again driving me crazy. After my parents go to bed, I sneak down to the basement and chug five or six big swallows from a bottle of vodka my father thought he'd hidden when he'd squirreled it away in the back of an armoire in the living room. In a short time, the bottle is only half full.

I fall asleep with my head reeling. Images of the psychiatric ward are getting hazier. I have a dim awareness that despite my honest desire to change, my absolute need to change, I won't be able to.

Something else is going to have to happen. And happen soon.

Chapter 5

MANY YEARS BEFORE my narrow escape from the psychiatric ward, my mind begins to play terribly cruel tricks on my body. My life changes forever sometime before my fifth birthday, with a simple shake of my head. Just like that.

It starts as I'm playing a video game. I feel an unusual, intense tension building up in my neck, and I think the only way to relieve it is to jerk my head to one side. A little while later, the tension is back and I do it again.

Soon my head is twisting more and more often, and the muscles in my neck are beginning to cramp.

I'm starting to get scared. Remember, I'm not quite five years old at the time. I'm just a little kid.

I try to stop, but the more I hold back, the stronger I feel the need to do it. My parents are looking at me, wondering what's going on.

That makes three of us.

When I wake up the next day, my head shaking is more or less a continuous thing. By lunchtime I know that my mother and father are worried because they aren't talking as much as they usually do.

By the following afternoon, the three of us are on our way to see a doctor. My father is driving pretty fast, and it feels as if we're in a speeding ambulance. At first I think it's my pediatrician we're going to see, but it's not.

"Is it going to hurt?" I want to know, stepping into an unfamiliar office.

"No, honey. This is a doctor who just wants to talk to you. This is a *talking* doctor."

In her office, Dr. Laufton asks me a lot of questions, such as "Do you ever feel like you have extra energy?"

"I guess so," I answer, because I think that's what she wants to hear.

Looking back, I realize this wasn't a good question. How could a kid my age have any idea what extra energy feels like?

"Why do you think you shake your head so much?" she asks after that.

Just thinking about it makes the shaking more violent. "I don't know. It feels like it wants me to," I say in between head thrusts.

That evening, my mother gives me a little pill to take. It's called Ritalin. I fall asleep pretty fast, but in the middle of the night I wake up feeling very restless and frightened.

I have no way of knowing it at the time, but Dr. Laufton has guessed wrong on the condition that's making my head shake. And she didn't realize that giving me Ritalin was like trying to put out a fire by drowning it in gasoline.

Chapter 6

AFTER TWO DAYS on Ritalin, I wake up having to move different parts of my face all the time — my nose, ears, forehead, cheeks, tongue.

Every few seconds, I squeeze my eyes shut until they hurt, then open them as wide as I can, then repeat this over and over. In the bathroom, I can't stop looking at myself in the mirror and distorting my face into the most grotesque expressions I can possibly make. I don't find the faces funny, just weird.

It's obvious that whatever was controlling me before has only been worsened by the medicine. For some reason, though, the urge to twist my head is gone. For now, anyway.

A day or two later, I'm in the kitchen and I'm about to eat breakfast with my sister, Jessie. Jessie is only eight months older than I am. My parents adopted her when my mom thought she couldn't have children of her own. Then Mom got pregnant with me *that same week.* Jessie may be only a little older than I am, but she's years ahead of me in just about every other way.

This morning I'm thinking about armies of bugs and germs. So there I am at breakfast, getting extremely disgusted by the idea that they could get inside my body somehow.

Then I see a big hairy horsefly buzzing overhead.

"Get it away from me!" I yell to anyone who can help. "Get it away, get it away!"

"Do you know what flies do every time they land?" Jessie says to me.

"What?"

"Throw up or go to the bathroom."

I'm so disgusted by this thought that as the fly lands near my plate, I start gagging.

My mother sees me and tries to swat the fly with a dishcloth, but she misses. The idea of its insect guts being smeared on the countertop makes me almost throw up again, and I beg her not to kill the fly.

"Please, Mommy, *don't!*" I screech.

Still, I'm very hungry. Last night the spaghetti Mom served made me think of a bunch of long, skinny white worms, and I went to bed without eating supper.

Jessie lifts a forkful of pancakes dripping with maple syrup, and I get past my bug thoughts long enough to do the same.

Enjoying her meal, she turns to me to see if I like it as much as she does. So there's absolutely no reason why, without any warning, I spit my mouthful of pancakes right in her face.

Jessie is so shocked that she just sits there, covered with food. Then she starts screaming.

"Don't do that again," my mother scolds loudly. "Tell your sister you're sorry."

I should feel bad, but instead I'm mostly fascinated with the impact of my spitting.

"Sorry, Jessie." Then I repeat, "Sorry, Jessie."

For some reason the word *sorry* stays in my mind. I want to say *sorry* again.

"Sorry. Sorry. Sorry, Jessie. Sorry, sorry, sorry."

Repeating the same word over and over makes everyone even more angry at me.

After a while Jessie calms down and we continue to eat, but the urge strikes again, and I can't help spitting another mouthful of pancakes at her.

This time her earsplitting scream brings my father running—and when he leans in to scold me, I spit right in his face, too. He's so surprised, he doesn't know what to do, except wipe his face with a towel.

"You'll have to leave the kitchen," my mother says, more serious than I've ever heard her. Actually, she looks more worried than angry. She doesn't understand why I'm doing this spitting thing any more than I do.

Instead of listening to her, I reach for more food to do it again. She takes the plate away just in time.

"Sorry, Dad. Sorry. Sorry, Mom. Sorry, Jessie. Sorry."

"That's the worst thing you can do to people," my father tells me, still dabbing wet spots on his cheeks. "The *worst*, Cory."

"Sorry, Dad. Sorry," I say, making a silly face.

I jump off my chair and take off to the family room, hooting as I run. I can't understand what's happening or what I'm doing. I love my family and would never spit at them.

This isn't me.

So who is it?

Chapter 7

AFTER I'VE SPENT a few more days on Ritalin, the totally new things I feel compelled to do keep shocking all of us.

And they change from day to day.

My parents tell Dr. Laufton they want me to stop taking the drug, but she says we have to give it a chance to work and allow my body time to adjust to it. I think that if the doctor had to live in my body *for even a few minutes,* she'd never give out that advice again.

Later that week at dinner, my father is at my side, showing me how to use my knife and fork.

"You feeling better today?" he asks.

Right away I answer, "You feeling better today?"

"No, I'm serious," he tries again. "How are you doing, Cory? I want to know."

"No, I'm serious. How are you doing?" I repeat back to him. "I want to know."

"Please don't do that," he says.

"Please don't do that," I answer, even though I don't want to. I want to talk to him about normal stuff, but instead I've made him angry with this stupid new habit of becoming a human echo.

Later on, when anybody tries to talk to me, I repeat their words before they can even finish the sentence. When I do this for the fifth or sixth time with my father, he gets up and walks away from me, just shaking his head. There's an expression on his face that I've never seen before, more like sadness than anger. My father's feelings always show on his face.

The next day, Jessie and I are in the TV room and I have a new urge: clearing my throat. The sound I make is halfway between a grunt and a low-pitched musical note.

After she's had enough, Jessie gets up to leave rather than start another fight. But as she passes by, I have to touch her on the shoulder.

"Don't do that, Cory," she says.

I touch her again several times at even intervals until something inside me feels satisfied.

"Get away from me," she yells.

I run after her, touching her shoulder again. *Two* taps, a pause, then *three* taps to make the feeling of having to do it go away. Her yelling gets my mother's attention and gets me a time-out.

"Sorry, Jessie. Sorry. Sorry, Jessie," I begin repeating like some kind of broken record.

Alone in my room, I pound my head with my fists to make it stop doing these things.

The next morning, I hear a song on my stereo, and when it's over I can't stop hearing the melody. It pushes out all other thoughts until I can't concentrate on anything else.

Later on that day, I hear a silly word in a cartoon and have to say the word over and over to everyone I come across. *Gooneybird. Gooneybird. Gooneybird.* I've begun to flap my arms like a bird, too, and I run around the house doing it whenever I get excited.

Things are getting worse every day, not better like the doctor said.

Today I'm like a jack-in-the-box, with new surprises popping out at any given moment. I feel as if my body is filled with electricity, and when I go to bed I can't lie still, even though I'm exhausted from my body moving all day. After a while my mother gives me a dose of Benadryl to get me to sleep, then another when the first doesn't work. The two doses eventually knock me out.

Finally, Gooneybird sleeps.

Chapter 8

TWO WEEKS AFTER our first visit to Dr. Laufton, we're back in her office, but I can't sit still in my chair for ten seconds. The head shaking is back full force, plus a lot of extreme grimacing and blinking and God only knows what else I'm doing. Even I can't keep track of all my new movements.

Dr. Laufton closes the notebook she's been using and sits back in her chair. She talks about some medical stuff that I don't understand. But I catch a bunch of unusual words coming out of her mouth.

"When I saw Cory last time, I thought we were dealing with attention-deficit/hyperactivity disorder,

ADHD, especially after he told me about feeling so much energy."

"But not now?" my father asks in a sharp tone. He isn't a big fan of the Ritalin that's turned my mind into fruit salad.

The doctor doesn't like the sound of his voice. "Cory, would you like to go into the waiting room and play with some of the toys I have there? I think you'd enjoy that."

My mother tells me to go and that she'll be there in a few minutes.

Years later, my mother filled me in on what was said after I left. Dr. Laufton wanted to let my parents decide what and when to tell me, but she said that from what she saw, it was likely that I had Tourette's syndrome. The head twisting, the grimacing, the spitting—they were all tics. Vocalizing—making sounds such as throat clearing—was another common symptom of Tourette's. *Echolalia* was the term for repeating other people's words.

The doctor said there was no quick fix to get rid of the condition, that my body needed to move on its own. But there were any number of medicines and combinations of medicines we might look into—it would be trial and error.

My mother and father didn't know it at the time, but they were about to go on a scary roller-coaster ride that would last for many years.

I already knew what the ride would be like.

I was on it — *and I was in the front seat.*

Chapter 9

I don't remember much about nursery school; mostly my teacher yells at me to do things I've forgotten to do and to *stop fidgeting*.

There are constant time-outs when I can't do simple things fast enough, such as hang my coat on a hook. My teacher is always mad at me, even though my mother tells her I can't help what I do. The teacher says my mother is overprotective and that she should go have another child and leave me to her. The truth is that in addition to my body movements, I was also born about seven weeks' premature and therefore am not as good with my motor skills as most kids are at that age.

By the time that long, excruciating spring and summer finally end and I arrive at kindergarten, it is obvious to my parents that my condition is actually several conditions. It is their choice not to tell me or anyone else the names of them. Tourette's syndrome isn't something people understand much about. It just makes you weird to other people.

And to yourself.

In first grade, my behavioral problems are a lot easier to see. My body is doing strange things several times a minute, and it has to be obvious to everyone that there is something very unusual about this kid named Cory.

My parents have found a new therapist for me. Her name is Dr. Pressler, and she is one of the world's leading experts in Tourette's syndrome.

The drive to meet Dr. Pressler takes about an hour and a half, because her office is in a medical building in another state.

After examining me, she puts me on a different medicine that's actually for people who have high blood pressure, but she says it helps a lot of Tourette's kids. Pretty much all the kids like me start off on clonidine.

When my behavior and my movements don't get much better, Dr. Pressler slightly increases the dose every few days, like my other doctor did. Clonidine definitely tires me out, so I don't have as much energy. But it doesn't stop me from twitching and jerking my arms and legs, or even from spitting at kids in school, which I've done off and on since my Ritalin days.

Some of the things I'm doing may not even be tics at all. Lately I *have* to stab paper cups with pens and knives, and I *have* to wash my hands several times after I use my computer. These compulsions don't feel the same as the other tics.

Then suddenly I start something new that happens every morning before school.

As my mother creeps ahead in a long line of cars to get to the entrance of the Dellbrook School, I get obsessed with the thought that something terrible is going to happen to her after she drops me off and I'm not around to protect her.

She's going to fall down a flight of stairs and die.
She'll be hit by a car or fall into a ditch.
Unless... unless...

Suddenly I think of the one thing that can save her, my mom's only hope.

"Promise you'll be first in line to pick me up?"

It doesn't matter to me that this isn't a logical solution to my mom getting hurt after she drops me off. All I know is that the thought seems to take away my feeling of dread.

"I will if I can, Cory," she says, sounding very unsure about my plan. "I can try, but there are a lot of mothers who come here to pick up their kids. I don't know if I can always be first."

"But you *have* to do it — every day. *Every single day.* You *have* to."

I wait for her to answer and can see that she's trying hard to work it out.

"Okay, honey. I will," she agrees.

"You'll be first in line when school is out? Will I see your car right away?"

"Yes, Cory, I'll be first in line."

"Every day?"

"Every day."

"Even forever?"

"Yes, even forever."

Chapter 10

ONE DAY my worst fear comes true. Leaving school, I see a silver station wagon at the head of the line. A wave of horror shoots through my body. *She's not here. Something happened to Mommy!*

I know that any second a teacher will come to tell me the bad news. She's been hit by an airplane that fell from the sky. Or there was a terrible car accident. I start crying uncontrollably, shaking horribly.

Then I see my mother in the distance, pulling up to the school quickly. She drives as close as she can and stops behind the silver wagon to be... *second in line!*

My mother rolls down the passenger window and yells for me to come, but I'm frozen in panic, still sobbing and shaking my head.

She yells again, but I still don't move.

A moment later, she steps on the gas and pulls around the silver car and ends up in a fire zone. Right away a crossing guard charges at her, as if she's just driven through the school's front window.

"You crossed the yellow line, lady. You have to move," he shouts loud enough for everyone in the pickup area to hear him.

By the time I'm running to her, she's surrounded by the crossing guard, a policeman on a bicycle, and a large, angry lady bus driver. In the middle of all the shouting and arguing, I dive into the car, and my mother takes off quickly.

On the way home, we don't talk about what just happened, and I don't really care anymore. I'm listening to a heavenly choir, singing words that thrill me.

She's alive, she's alive. My mommy's alive!

And I've made it through another day without my mother getting sucked down into a manhole.

Chapter 11

NO ONE CAN IMAGINE how horrible this is. Every single day, *something bad happens to me.*

A few steps from the front entrance to school, a spasm shakes my shoulders and freezes me in place. I jerk my chin straight up to the sky as high as it can go and lock it in that position for the next three or four seconds.

When the spasm finally stops, I take a few deep breaths to relax, but it happens *again,* then *again* a few steps later. I'm only six years old and don't know why my medicines aren't helping me by now.

Nothing is working. I'm actually getting worse.

I'm incredibly discouraged that the day is starting off with my tics being so bad. I like going to school, and my first-grade teacher, Mrs. Wilkens, has been nice to me so far. My mother was able to have an early conference with her, and she "gets" my problems and knows how to deal with me.

Mom is always having to explain me, not only to the teachers but to everyone who sees me acting funny. Once she clarifies the situation, people usually get over their shock. But not always.

I try not to look back at the car because I know that my mother is still watching and feeling bad for me. She always tries to hide how worried she is, but these days she doesn't look as happy as she used to. I wish I could stop being the way I am for her. She is the best mother anyone could ever have, and I love her so much.

School only makes my tics worse. There's no doubt about that. Now there are so many tics we've started to give them names. The *hopping tic,* the *bend-at-the-waist tic,* the *chin thrust,* the *scrunchy face.* When I began the *twisting tic,* I felt something rip in my back, but I still had to keep doing it. I had to go to the hospital and be drugged asleep in order to make it stop. I never thought the twisting tic would end, but it did after a few days.

My tics keep changing all the time. They started mostly in my neck and face, but now they are all over my body and affect my large-muscle movements. There doesn't seem to be any limit to how many kinds there are.

I do the chin thrust a few more times before getting to the front door of my school. The pressure is so strong on my spine it feels like it's about to snap. This is not such a wild thought. I already know that my tics can make me hurt myself. Before I ripped the muscle in my back, I was biting down so hard on a bottom tooth that I broke it in half and had to be rushed to the dentist. The dentist didn't believe what had actually happened.

Even though I'm trying hard to be good, this day gets off to a terrible start. During the spelling lesson, Mrs. Wilkens asks me to write the "word of the day" on the blackboard, and I feel proud to have been selected. I can tell she likes me, even though I tic a lot in class and require some extra work on her part.

When I get to the front of the class, Mrs. Wilkens pronounces the word of the day and asks me to write it.

My writing isn't very good because I have trouble holding the chalk and forming the letters, but I always try my best to please her. And everybody else.

Before I start, I sound out the word in my mind,

the way she told us to do. Then I turn to the black-board and get the chalk ready.

But instead of writing the word of the day, my hand writes the word SHIT in great big letters.

For a moment I stand there, staring at the word in horror and shame.

I don't know what just happened, only that something told me to do it. I know it's one of the worst things I could have done, and I'm as shocked as anyone.

As soon as the kids see the word, they start laughing and pointing at the blackboard. I'm so embarrassed, I want to erase it, but I can't.

"Sorry," I say to Mrs. Wilkens. "Sorry. Sorry."

My face contorts, and my eyes close and open fast and tight. Not only have I written a bad word on the blackboard but it's making my tics worse. The combination of what I've written and my silly faces starts the other kids laughing harder and louder. Mrs. Wilkens isn't laughing at all. She's angry.

"Everyone be quiet," she shouts. *"Cory, take your seat. Now."*

"Sorry," I say again, but I don't think she's listening.

Then I get the idea that it will be better if I make it look like I'm doing everything on purpose, as a joke. The kids will think that I'm funny and not just weird.

So I make a few more silly faces, including a dopey grin. This makes the kids laugh again. I laugh along with them.

Mrs. Wilkens yells at us again, and this time the room goes completely silent.

I get to my seat and slip into it quietly. Inside, I'm feeling so bad that I let Mrs. Wilkens down when she trusted me at the blackboard. But I also realize for the first time that I can get kids to laugh *with* me instead of *at* me when I do something inappropriate. I can become the class clown.

One thing is for sure. From this day on, I can't go to my classroom without thinking about writing SHIT or some other bad word. And I live in paralyzing fear of going up to the blackboard again.

Chapter 12

I'M MAKING IT very hard for my mother to drive. We're coming home from the YMCA, where she's taken me to play basketball with some kids like me who don't have much else to do or other kids to play with.

We're on a narrow country road, and the traffic is bad. My mother is trying to make a left turn at an intersection, but there's another car coming at us, and she has to decide if she can make it in time.

Already on this ride I've been sticking my head out the window and also making silly faces in the rear-view mirror, like I used to do in my bathroom. This is getting my mother upset, but not as upset as when I need to *open my door while the car is moving.*

The reason I'm so wild today may be the new medicine I'm on. I'm getting anxious about starting third grade only a few weeks from now, so my doctor is trying a new drug called Haldol. This one was made for people with problems such as schizophrenia and big mood changes.

The Haldol is already having a bad effect, making me do strange, risky things—like now, when we're driving.

Just as my mother is about to turn left, I have an urge to do something new that is unexpectedly dangerous. I suddenly touch the steering wheel and push it to the right.

When my mother feels the wheel turning out of her control, she pushes my hand away.

"Cory, you could cause an accident!"

This makes me want to touch the wheel even more, but I just tap it in a teasing, slightly threatening way.

All the while, an oncoming car is getting closer. By now I've distracted my mother so much that when she faces the road again, she has to make a faster decision.

She steps on the gas pedal, but I can see she's so upset, she's made a mistake. The car is coming at us too fast. We're not going to get out of the way in time, and it's too late to stop.

"Mom!" I call out. "Mom! Mom!"

My mother tries to speed up, but the oncoming car is right next to us. It slides sideways as the driver hits the brakes and tries to steer around us.

A thunderous crash rocks our car. It lifts the front end right off the ground. Suddenly I'm flying forward. My head slams hard into the windshield with a loud crunching sound. I see a blinding white flash, then little lights sparkle in my eyes.

"Mom?" I cry out in pain and confusion.

Chapter 13

WHEN EVERYTHING STOPS moving, there's smoke spewing from the engine of the car that hit us, blowing crazily over the hood. A young woman pries open the door and steps out, crying and stumbling over her feet.

I'm dizzy from the hit against the windshield. I look over at my mother to see how she is.

Her head is resting on the steering wheel. I think she's hurt very badly, and I know it's because of me. But then she pushes herself back up and lets out a breath. She looks at me in wonder, then at the windshield. She sees the broken glass.

"Cory, are you all right?" she asks. I can tell she's very afraid. I've never loved her more than I do right now. She's so precious to me.

"I guess so," I say, trying to be brave.

"Does your head hurt?"

She touches a large swelling on my forehead that I hadn't noticed. Now I can feel it pulsing, but there's no pain yet and it's not bleeding.

"I don't know why the air bags didn't go off to keep you away from the windshield," Mom says.

And I don't know why I needed to touch the steering wheel.

Chapter 14

WHEN THE PHONE RINGS, I look away from the video game and listen to hear who's calling. I hope that my mother will shout my name and tell me that it's a friend who wants to play—but, as usual, it isn't. Fourth graders are pretty much staying away from me nowadays. My tics are driving me and everyone else crazy.

Even Jessie is keeping her distance, and we're usually pretty close. A few days ago, I was in the front seat of our car and suddenly hurled myself over the backrest and landed on top of her. I hurt her so much that she screamed in pain. I feel so bad when I have to do things like that to her. Jessie used to try to calm me down and hug me when I got restless, but now there are too many things I do that threaten her, and she can't trust me anymore.

My father is spending more time with me, probably to make up for my not having any friends.

One afternoon, my father and I are in the basement putting together a new model car with a real gas engine. The car has hundreds of tiny parts, and he's helping me find one that's missing. After looking for a while, I'm suddenly aware of how close our heads are. The fact that they're almost touching gives me an urge to do something wild and inappropriate, like spit in his face. *Something is telling me to ruin our good time.*

Out of nowhere the F word flies into my mind. It's the worst word I can say, like the time I wrote SHIT on the blackboard at school. I try hard to hold back from saying it, but when the urge becomes overpowering, I lose the fight. Only it comes out as *fu fu fu fu fu,* as though I'm stuttering.

My father knows right away what I'm almost saying.

"What's that about?" he wants to know with a disappointed expression.

"I'm not sure. It just came out."

"Where did you hear that word?"

"Nowhere . . . I guess."

He starts to tell me not to do it anymore but then stops short. He knows the first rule: telling me not to do something only makes me want to do it more.

"Sorry, Dad. Sorry. Sorry, Dad."

"That's okay, don't worry about it," he says. Shifting topics, he goes on, "Have you seen anything that looks like this?" He points to a picture of a part in the car instructions.

"Fu fu fu fu fu," I answer.

"I bet it's in here somewhere," he says, ignoring the near curse and digging into a new pile of loose screws and plastic pieces.

I guess I'm lucky that I almost never feel the urge to curse in front of people like some kids do, and that when I start to, I can usually control it. If you have to curse out loud, you can't be in a regular classroom or go to the movies or restaurants because people don't understand. Just like when I give people the bird. No matter how many times my mother or father explains that I can't help it, they don't believe it.

My father's distractions help me forget the F word, and we spend a happy time putting most of the car together.

"How'd you get so good at this?" he says when we're done for the day.

"Dunno," I answer proudly.

But I do. I can spend hours at a time doing something I love because it becomes an obsession. Sometimes obsessions can work for you.

In bed that night, I can feel the medicine helping my mind shut down. I think about what a mostly good day I had with my father, and then I remember the one thing that wasn't so good.

Fu fu fu fu fu, I say softly into the darkness. *Fu fu fu fu fu.*

I don't think this is a regular tic. It's more like a thought I have to act on. Or maybe that's the same thing. And I suddenly recall where I first got the idea of having to say bad things and having no control over it.

Our family had recently watched a comedy that made fun of different kinds of people with terrible conditions. One was a woman who kept cursing out loud, and she explained that it was because she had Tourette's syndrome. I remember being so surprised.

"Does Tourette's make people say bad words?" I whispered to my father.

He looked really angry, but not at me.

"No, this is a bad movie, Cory. They make fun of people who can't help themselves, and they shouldn't."

And that was the way I learned about the cursing tic. It's called *coprolalia*.

I go to sleep wondering why grown-ups would want to make a movie that pokes fun at people who can't help themselves. And I wonder if they still would if there was somebody in their own family like me.

Chapter 15

IT FEELS STRANGE and almost wrong to see the hallways so empty and silent at this time of day in such a big school.

I'm late for class because the extra Benadryl I needed to take last night made me oversleep. It's the end of fourth grade, and it's getting harder to stay in school for the whole day, but I want to try. Yesterday I was twitching and jumping around so much that my shirt was soaking wet by sixth period.

On the way to class, I see three girls around my age whom I haven't noticed before. They use the word *like* about ten times in five seconds. *And I, like, go with him, and, like, oh my God! That's, like, so awesome.*

I wonder—do they have tics? Is saying *like* really a tic? If so, I know an awful lot of other kids who have it.

As they pass by me, I bend at the waist and jerk my head to one side. The girls stop their conversation and smile as they go by, but after they're farther down the hall, I can hear them giggling. I don't know if it's because of me or something else.

Still, I feel pretty good about being in school today. I don't know if it's my new medicine or not. I've been completely off Haldol for a while, and Dr. Pressler has replaced it with Cogentin. This is yet another medicine made for something else, in this case for people with Parkinson's disease. Parkinson's sufferers have problems with the way their bodies move, so I guess that's a good reason to try it on me.

Dr. Pressler will do anything to help. She's very disappointed that she hasn't found a great medicine for me like she has for hundreds of other children.

So far Cogentin is better than Haldol. Or maybe it's just that the Haldol is wearing off. I never know. A lot of my wild behavior has stopped, especially the feeling that I might need to curse. Haldol gave me an unbelievable appetite. Now my body is doing some new things. I guess that could just be a sign of getting worse as I get older.

The real problem is that it's hard to know what's causing what, with everything going on at the same time. There are all the different medicines with different doses and combinations, and the time of year. Spring usually seems to be the worst. Then there is the stress of school and of the way Tourette's always changes, getting worse, then better, then worse again. It's called *waxing and waning*. With all this, none of my doctors have been able to figure out precisely what's going on, so whenever they prescribe a new medicine, it's always just a guess.

The best thing about school this year is my teacher, Mrs. Erlanger. She never ever lets the other kids make fun of me. She's explained to them that just because my body moves, it doesn't mean there's anything wrong with me, and that it's no big deal.

Today I promise to be extra good in class for her. Today I'm going to be a "Tourette's angel."

Chapter 16

BY THE END OF THE MORNING, things are going well. Mrs. Erlanger has called on me almost every time I've raised my hand. She praises me a lot and never lets my ticcing bother her. She tells my mother that she loves the way I always contribute in class. I can't tell you how great that makes me feel—like I'm a regular kid.

Things change at lunch.

I see my two old neighborhood friends sitting alone at a table, and there's an empty seat next to them. I sit down and say hi. They look at each other, then just get up and leave. They never say anything; they just take off. I feel so bad I can't stand it. They go to sit with their other friends.

After that I don't want to try to sit with anyone. Most of the time I eat alone anyway, except now and then I sit with William. He's a nice kid who doesn't seem to have friends either. William has learning disabilities.

Eating by myself isn't that terrible, mainly because I love the food my mother packs for me. Today my lunch box is stuffed with all my favorites — fruit salad, cookies, and sandwiches my mother makes herself.

Back in class, Mrs. Erlanger is slowly reciting a poem for us and wants us to print it out as she speaks, but I'm having trouble. The pencil is clumsy in my hand, and I need my words to be *exactly* on the blue line, not even a little above or below. I also need my letters to be *perfectly* formed, and since I can never get it right the first time, I have to erase and start over. I'm doing that so much today that I've made holes in my papers. I hate the sloppy holes so much.

Soon I'm so far behind that out of frustration I break my pencil in two and stop working. I've been breaking pencils in two all the time lately, at home and in school, even when I'm not using them to write. I don't know why. I just do it.

To try and relax, I begin to drum my fingers on my desk. I drum out a series of beats over and over, so after a while it attracts attention.

Mrs. Erlanger looks up and sees that it's me, then gives me a little smile and goes back to her reading.

One of the good things she's done for me is to make me the class messenger. This is a job the other kids want since it gets them out of class for some free time. When Mrs. Erlanger sees that I'm getting a little out of control, she usually says, *I need someone to go to the office for me. Cory, would you mind?* So while everyone else continues studying, I get to leave before I disrupt the class any further, and I go chill out in the nurse's office.

As I keep up my drumming, Mrs. Erlanger seems to be getting annoyed. I guess it can get on anyone's nerves after a while. It even gets on mine.

I soon realize that I'm getting stuck on drumming, and I stuff my hand in my pocket to stop. *I'm trying so hard to be good.*

I look around and I see a kid named Jerome grinning at me. He sits a few seats away and is one of the boys who likes to get me in trouble.

When I stop drumming, he makes a low chirping sound that I can hear but the teacher can't. It's similar to one of my throat tics, and thinking about it makes me start doing it, which is just what Jerome wants.

Soon I chirp loud enough for the other kids to hear, and I make a silly face so it looks like I'm doing it on purpose — the class clown again.

Now I'm chirping so much a bunch of the boys start to imitate me, and that does it for Mrs. Erlanger. She jumps out of her chair with an angry look I haven't seen before.

"This is not funny. I need you *all* to be quiet. Do you understand?"

The room gets so quiet that I can hear somebody outside mowing a lawn. At first I'm relieved that the laughing has stopped, but then the silence gets to me and becomes its own problem. I need to do something to break it. I know this is a terrible time to make a noise, but that's what the urge is all about.

Finally it gets so strong I can't stop it. My throat makes another chirp, then another one, even louder.

The class holds its breath, waiting for Mrs. Erlanger's next reaction.

"I think it would help if you could control that, Cory," she says in a sharp, slightly strained voice.

I can't believe it. *Are you asking me to stop?* She knows I can't control it, and telling me to only increases my need to do it. I feel like I've suddenly been attacked by the only person in school I can trust.

The tension makes me chirp again, even louder,

and now I'm stuck in a terrible cycle I can't get out of.

"I think a time-out will do us all some good!" Mrs. Erlanger shouts over the noise. "Cory, why don't you spend a few minutes outside in the hall?" she says, and points to the door.

Her order stuns me. I'm supposed to be a messenger when this happens, not punished. Everyone knows the hall is punishment. I'm confused and hurt, *really hurt.*

I get up to leave and grab my book bag without looking at it, but the bag is open and all my books and papers spill around me on the floor. This starts another round of laughter from my classmates.

Nothing is making any sense. My favorite teacher is mad at me and she's making me act worse. My classmates are provoking me into doing things they can make fun of. I'm lost and embarrassed and ticcing wildly. I'm so afraid, I can't stand it.

Then I realize that another bad feeling is starting up inside of me.

I'm beginning to get angry. Very angry.

Chapter 17

I LOVE MY SISTER—she's my best friend—but sometimes it's so hard for us, unbelievably hard and unfair. I can cause her a lot of trouble and pain, and every now and then she starts to get even.

I don't know why she picked tonight to try to trick me. It's bad enough that a new tic is making me twist my shoulders so hard that the bed creaks. Add this to all my other nightly thrashing around, and my bedposts are getting wobbly enough to collapse.

But just as the clonidine and Benadryl are finally beginning to work, I hear Jessie from her bedroom, which is right next to mine.

"'Night, Cory," she sings out a little too happily, and my eyes pop open.

There are certain phrases people say to me that I *always* have to respond to. Saying *good night* is one of them, and Jessie knows it.

"'Night, Jessie," I say as quickly as I can, trying to make it sound as if it's the last time we'll be doing this.

I'm about to drift off when she does it again.

"'Night, Cory."

"Stop doing that, Jessie!" I yell back, and quickly follow it up with another "'Night, Jessie."

This isn't like her. Jessie is almost always on my side, but lately things are changing. She used to let me join in when her friends came over to play, but now she takes them right to her room and locks the door. I guess it's hard for her to have a brother like me when she's trying to be regular.

Yesterday she deliberately got me in trouble. When my mother wasn't around, she told me that it was okay to pee in the bathroom sink. And when I did, she told on me.

It's easy for Jessie to trick me, just like she's doing tonight. She's smart and plans ahead much better than I do. A while back, she made up a rule that whoever yells *Front seat* first gets it when we go for a ride.

I agreed because I thought I'd always remember, but so far she's won about a hundred times in a row. Occasionally she remembers to call *Front seat* when we're still in the house. And every time she wins, she laughs in triumph.

I stay awake for a long time, waiting for Jessie to say it again, which is just as bad as her doing it, but finally, when nothing more happens, the medicine takes over and I drift off into...

" 'Night, Cory."

The gleeful little call splits open the darkness, and I sit up in bed and yell for my mother, who shows up fast.

"What's the matter, Cory? Are you all right?"

"Jessie won't stop saying ' 'Night, Cory.' She's doing it on purpose."

Mom ducks into Jessie's room and scolds her until she promises to stop.

Finally, sleep arrives, and with it my best dream. I'm riding a motorcycle on a highway that goes on forever. I'm traveling faster and faster, bent down over the handlebars, passing everyone else. I'm not thinking about anything as the cars and trees fly past—except the thrill that's rippling through my body.

Eventually I'm going so fast that my motorcycle races ahead of the sound of its roaring engine, and

I'm moving in a state of blissful quiet, as if I'm the only one at the very tip of a spaceship. A wonderful voice talks to me, telling me that this is how happy I will be someday. *This blessed freedom will be mine.*

And then comes another voice, from another place and time, a softer one, just loud enough for me to hear.

" 'Night, Cory."

Part Two

ONWARD AND DOWNWARD

Chapter 18

I STARE UP at the two-hundred-year-old tree in my backyard, almost out of breath from the excitement. It's more than a hundred feet tall. I wonder how many storms it must have survived to still be here, waiting for a barefoot kid with an unusual urge to climb.

The tree trunk has to be at least twenty feet around and looks like a huge elephant's foot. I wonder if I'm really crazy to be doing this, but I don't think so. *Crazy* is someone who kills people because his dog tells him to.

I have to climb because there's no other way to get rid of the urge that's building up inside me. It's as if I have wires in my brain that light up at the thought of it, but they're wired to the wrong places and don't allow the electricity to turn off.

So this isn't about being crazy. This is about bad wiring.

Right now I should be at school with the other fifth graders, but today I can't sit still long enough to make it through the whole day.

So this afternoon, while the other kids are learning English, geography, and math, my assignment is climbing.

Lucky for me, the kids who lived here before left a homemade rope ladder that's still attached to the first branch. I stand on the rope step and can tell it's strong enough to hold me.

I hook my foot around the next rung, but right away my leg shoots straight out and slams into the tree. This is what I'm most afraid of, the excitement making my body spark more than usual. A wrong move a hundred feet in the air will make the trip down a lot faster than the climb up.

On the next try, my leg is okay, and I keep going until I run out of ladder and can grab hold of the first branch and pull myself into the tree.

The next few branches line up one above the other, and I climb them quickly. Then a large gap stops me.

My bending tic hits all at once, and my stomach clenches so hard that for a few seconds I can hardly breathe. The thrust forward shifts my weight so much it throws me off balance, and *suddenly I'm falling.*

My whole body jerks to a stop when my legs get tangled in a thick bunch of branches and end my fall. It all happened so fast that I didn't have time to be scared, but I am now that it's over.

I stay very still and suck in a few gallons of air.

I look down and see just how bad an idea this whole thing was. Below, there's a pattern of small light and dark rectangles, and I realize they're the roof shingles on my house.

I'm much higher up than I thought, and I wonder how I'm going to get down.

That thought makes me *need* to test the danger of a fall. I let go of the limb I'm holding on to for just a second until I start to lose my balance. Then I grab it again at the last moment. I test again by letting go for a longer time and almost don't get my grip back before it's too late.

But I still need to climb. I wrap both arms around an overhead branch and hook one leg around it, then the other, and in a moment I'm hanging upside down.

All at once a big muscle in my left leg contracts,

making it straighten out. Now only one leg is attached to the tree, and *I'm still hanging upside down.*

I dangle there, high off the ground, not knowing if I'm going to fall. I wait for the spasm to stop, then I wrap my leg back around the branch and haul myself right side up.

I don't know how long I've been climbing. My shirt is soaked with sweat.

The muscles in my arms are tingling from the strain of holding on for so long, but being this close to the top elates me.

I push apart a final thick clump of leaves, and a small space opens up. Now I can see where some of the highest branches end. The branches here are thinner, and I don't know if the last one will hold my weight, but I'm not going back down until I find out.

I take a deep breath and go for it. It bends but doesn't break. *And I'm there!*

I actually begin to relax. The breeze is like a silk scarf on my skin. Far below, the earth looks like it's moving back and forth, but it's only the treetop swaying.

I'm like a bird in the canopy of a great forest — one that's washing stillness over my body. Up here, I'm part of another world — a zone without time or stress. I needed to get here because of the thrill but also because, up here, there's something I can never find on the ground. *A place where no one can see me tic.*

I don't see any reason to come down.

No reason in the world.

What I don't know, and won't for many years, is that the act of climbing this tree is the key to something wonderful.

This is it. I just don't know it yet.

Chapter 19

YOU'D HAVE TO BE unconscious not to realize that something is about to break loose in the Resource Room at my school. It's obvious to all the kids that Phillip is getting more hyper by the minute, but Mr. Jansen is still sitting behind his desk, reading today's *New York Times*. He seems concerned with what's going on only when it gets so loud that you can hear us in the halls or when someone starts to freak out. Then he yells, "Be quiet and sit down! Now!"

The Resource Room is a classroom set up as a quiet space for special-needs kids like me who require a break in order to get through the school day or need a place to go when they get to be too much to handle in a regular classroom. The teachers have started sending me here for time-outs a lot, ever since my behavior in class got out of control.

Everything about middle school has made me worse. Just changing classes puts me under unbelievable pressure. I can't work the combination on my locker very well, so I'm always late for my next period. When I finally do get the door open, I usually forget to lock it again. Already I've had my jacket, books, and several lunches stolen. Feeling anxious between classes makes me worry all the time, and that's made my tics go off the charts.

This is the main reason one of my teachers sent me to the Resource Room again today.

There aren't that many of us in the school who come here, and everybody knows who we are. I'm not the only sixth grader, but I'm the only one who comes because his body is like a Mexican jumping bean.

The trouble with the Resource Room is that it isn't what it's supposed to be — a rest. It's not really Mr. Jansen's fault. He can't do much to keep kids like us under control. We're already on medicines for that, and he probably figures that we come to this room when our medicines aren't working. What chance does he have?

So I'm not surprised when, without any warning, Phillip bursts out of his chair and begins to run around the room, screaming his lungs out and knocking things off other kids' desks and the blackboard railing. Phillip is the most out-of-control kid in the entire school. He never stops moving and can't be quieted down no matter what people say to him. So Phillip and I have a lot in common.

On his second lap around the classroom, Phillip suddenly cuts into a row of desks and slides to a stop within a few inches of a boy named Danny. You never know what Danny is going to do either. He can be as still as a rock, just staring into space, or he can get as wild and crazy as Phillip.

Phillip approaches Danny and reaches for his head, grabbing a fistful of curly red hair. Before Danny knows what's happening, he's being dragged out of his chair headfirst. Even though he's way off balance, he manages to get to his feet and kick Phillip in the leg. He follows that by grabbing Phillip's arm and sinking his teeth into Phillip's wrist.

Phillip retaliates with a kick of his own that misses Danny and makes a desk go flying. Both kids are about the same size, so this fight could go on for a while, unless the teacher gets them to stop.

"Hey, you two!" Mr. Jansen yells, making his way

into the fight. He reaches Danny just in time to stop him from pushing his hand into Phillip's face. The teacher separates them by grabbing their shirt collars.

"Knock it off right now or you're going to Mr. Arno's office."

The threat of being sent to see Mr. Arno scares just about everybody in the school. Mr. Arno is the vice principal and is in charge of discipline. He's a big man with a floppy mustache and an expression like that of a snarling wolf. When he talks, he sounds like he's barking at you.

Phillip doesn't tune in to what Mr. Jansen is saying, so he continues to fight until his shirt is almost torn off his back.

Danny is more in touch with reality. He stops fighting, which calms Phillip down. In a few seconds, Phillip stomps back to his seat.

Mr. Jansen shakes a finger at both of them. "Don't make me talk to you again. This is a rest period. *All you have to do is be quiet!*"

For a while things are peaceful, but Danny is still upset. Phillip has really hurt him this time, and he's angry.

All of a sudden, Danny lets out a howl and launches himself like a missile at Phillip. He knocks both Phillip and his desk backward.

"That's it!" Mr. Jansen hollers, charging out of his seat again.

I want to help calm things down, mainly for Danny's sake—he didn't do anything to deserve being attacked. But the last time I tried to help in a situation like this, I was told to stay in my seat, and I don't want to make Mr. Jansen angry at me.

The fight ends before the teacher gets to them. Danny has satisfied his urge for revenge and is moving back to his seat. Phillip is also tired of the fight—the last push knocked him out of his chair and sent him sprawling to the floor.

For the first time since I came into the Resource Room today, there's no noise. The quiet feels good, but it's already too late for me. I'm more anxious now than I was when I got here.

The silence lasts about another twenty seconds. Without warning, Phillip leaps out of his desk and heads full force for Danny, waving his arms and offering up an earsplitting scream.

Mr. Jansen bolts out of his chair again, but before he gets to them, the fight spills over to where two other kids are sitting. One is the only girl in the room, and she starts crying and puts her head down on her desk.

I put my head down, too, to try to block out what's

going on. I make a few throat-clearing sounds and do a few shoulder lurches that have been building up. Poor Mr. Jansen doesn't know what to do or who to talk to first, so he ends up standing there, checking the clock on the wall. He still has ten minutes left with us.

My mom has to come early to pick me up, *but at least she's first in the car line.*

Chapter 20

WHAT'S SO TERRIBLY WRONG with me that so many smart people can't help me figure a way out of it? It's been *more than six years* since my body started jerking, shaking, quivering, twitching, and exploding on its own. I'm more out of control than ever, and I wonder why anyone thinks another drug is going to help after we've tried so many. I'm already eleven years old. My so-called childhood is almost gone.

Lately I've heard Dr. Pressler describe some of the things I do as *compulsions*. That's why she's prescribed Celexa, the first antidepressant I've ever taken. Everyone thinks it could be a breakthrough for me, since antidepressants work on compulsions, but in my case, the medicine seems to make everything worse. Celexa hypes up the need to jerk my body to one side so violently that I hurt a nerve or something, and it takes days for me to stop jerking and hurting myself.

After Celexa comes Paxil, another antidepressant. My doctor says it's worth trying because different medicines can do different things, even if they're in the same general category.

For a while Paxil really helps my mood. I become much happier than before, and being happy calms my tics down. But then my mood gets so good that it doesn't feel real. I actually tell my mother, "I don't want to grow up. I don't want things to change." *How weird is that?*

The good time doesn't last for very long, anyway. By the end of a week of nirvana, I start getting into trouble at school again, falling off chairs and being disruptive. So my mother begins to take me off Paxil right away. *Against medical advice,* I guess. A short while later, the school calls her and says I had a great day, and she thinks that my getting off Paxil is the reason. But I think, *If things are better when I'm off Paxil, then why weren't they better when I wasn't on it to begin with?* Maybe it's only that I'm still coming off the drug, which is like being on a lower dose. So we go up and down on Paxil a few more times, but we can't see that it helps, and I finally get off it altogether.

When I have good and then bad days on the same medicine, it's hard to know what's going on. Is the medicine wearing off? Is it the different doses I'm trying? Dr. Pressler says maybe my mind eventually figures out how to beat each medicine so that it can go back to the way it was.

Fluvoxamine is one of the worst drugs I try because its side effects are so extreme. At first it calms me down quickly. My dose is increased, and I have another great day at school. Right after that I can't stop laughing in art class and am asked to leave.

From there I become depressed, and the dose goes up again. Three more calm days in school are followed by a sudden burst of more tics and cursing in front of friends. I begin clenching and unclenching my right hand so hard that after a while it becomes impossible to open and close it at all.

Even worse, my body is jerking almost continuously, and for the first time it keeps doing it in my sleep, the only period when my body gets a rest. That's a real problem. I can't sleep, and it's making me crazy, seriously crazy.

When we finally lower the dose of fluvoxamine, my twitching goes down pretty fast; the cursing, too. My food and germ phobias go away. Then we add clonidine, which I have taken since first grade, and everything is okay until I start throwing things and having to touch boiling pots of water on the stove. I get in trouble at school by talking, laughing uncontrollably, and saying nasty things, so there goes fluvoxamine.

It kills me that there are so many unsolved mysteries about my medicines. Once in a while one starts to work, then something changes and the side effects get worse. I never know if it's the medicine itself, the combination of medicines, the doses, or the usual ups and downs that happen with Tourette's. This is the most complicated puzzle I can imagine for my doctors and parents to try to figure out — which probably explains why they haven't so far.

But we have no choice except to keep trying. Our new plan is to start on BuSpar in a few days, because Dr. Pressler now believes anxiety is causing everything else to be worse. She's also talking about trying a new drug called Risperdal, an antipsychotic used for schizophrenia and to control violent behavior. This is a very big decision for my parents. Risperdal hasn't typically been used for Tourette's, and I'll be one of the first Tourette's kids in America to try it. I'll also be part of a new study, like a lab rat.

Risperdal worries me for another reason. People who take it gain, on average, thirty-five to forty pounds. So instead of being just a kid who can't stop moving, I'll become a *fat* kid who can't stop moving.

Chapter 21

I'M STANDING on the pitcher's mound in front of hundreds of people in the biggest game of the year, the Little League town championship, on Memorial Day weekend. I'm basically a nervous wreck but also as happy as I've ever been. This is a rare chance for me to be the center of attention.

For the right reasons.

Playing baseball is the best time of my life, and against all odds I've become a good pitcher, a sixth grader who can throw a sixty-five-mile-per-hour fastball, though not always as straight as I would like.

I'm also able to hit long home runs when I'm not striking out, which happens a lot, too.

We're losing by three runs, and they've got the bases loaded with two outs in the fourth inning. I've just come in to replace our pitcher. My team expects my help in winning a game that will be talked about until next season's first practice sessions, when there's still snow on the ground. At least, in my family it will be talked about.

Today I've come to the game with many more tricky moves than the crowd expects. Due to the stress, my tics and compulsions have reached a whole new level. I'm also bigger than anyone's ever seen me. As expected, I've gained thirty-five pounds from the Risperdal, which I've been on for a few months.

And I've taken an extra dose before today's game.

As the stadium quiets and I look for a signal from the catcher, I give in to an urge to start touching the tip of my nose with my mitt in an exact sequence, three times, then two times, then one. I complete this complex compulsion by tapping myself softly in the crotch with my glove.

Today, because of the extra tension, I've done this ritual before each of my first two pitches, and it has distracted me so much that both pitches were balls, missing the strike zone by a mile.

This time when I start my tics, I notice some of the guys on the other team watching me from the sidelines. So far they aren't reacting, just staring. Even though I know they're aware of my Tourette's, I tell myself that a lot of pitchers, out of nervousness, go through their own rituals on the mound, even in the major leagues, so maybe what I'm doing is no big deal.

When the touching is over, I stand up straight and turn the ball in my glove until the stitches are in the exact right place for my fingers.

My body becomes still, I cock my right arm, and I throw the ball as hard as I can. It flies straight over the center of the plate so fast that the batter can't get around in time. The umpire calls *strike one*. I'm in heaven. *All right! There's hope.*

The crowd in the bleachers to my right is rooting for my team, and they erupt in a cheer like they've just witnessed the best thing ever. It's amazing to see how important this game is to them, and it feels good to know that I've come through with a decent pitch.

Nose three times, then two, then one, pound my crotch.

This time one of the kids from the other team picks up on my ritual of movements and yells, "What's the matter, pitcher, you nervous? Can't take the heat?"

I have a tough time concentrating on my next pitch. Then another kid shouts, "Choke, choke."

I take my foot off the rubber for a break, turn to the outfield, and try not to think about the cruel taunting and about what happened in my pregame warm-up. I'd been throwing really well, not every one a strike, but most. Then, all of a sudden, I let go of a ball that sailed at least ten feet over the practice catcher's head. Something told me, *Throw a wild pitch.*

I worry that this can happen now, in the real game.

I also worry that something will tell me to throw the ball at the batter, which would be horrible. I can't stand the thought of hurting anyone with my pitching. I do throw fast, and this hardball in my hand is a lethal weapon.

By now a bunch of the opposing team's players are off the bench and standing along the first-base line. The batter is taking warm-up swings at the plate.

The next time I touch my nose, I hear one of the players yell something at me, then another and another. Their voices echo in my head, and even though I can't get all the words, I know for sure that they're making fun of my ticcing and dancing around.

"Choke, choke, choke," they chant in unison.

They all know I can't help the tics, and I can't believe they're using it against me. This is really crummy sportsmanship. Why isn't someone telling them to stop? Where's their coach, a grown-up who has to know how unfair this is?

I hurry through the rest of my movements, just to stop the shouting, and throw a really bad pitch for ball three.

The other team bursts out laughing, like they know they've made me worse by taunting me. It's cruel and it's wrong, but it's working.

Even before I get ready for my next pitch, the whole team is shouting all kinds of things to make me more nervous.

I look for their coach again to see if he's going to stop this. He's the father of one of the players and also the team manager, and when I spot him I'm shocked to see that he's up on his feet next to them. He's yelling at me right along with his team. He's leading them on.

I don't know how a grown-up can be doing such a thing. It feels like he's using my nervousness against me. I thought everyone would have known what this would do to me.

The more they yell, the more I need to tic. Suddenly I lurch forward with a bending tic. When they see that, the noise level goes up even more. But not on my team's side of the stadium; they are mostly quiet.

I suddenly hear my father's voice rising above our opponents' shouting. I look over at him, and at my mother and sister. My father is standing now and calling across the infield to the other team's coach. He's telling him to shut his players up, but the coach isn't paying any attention. My mother is staying in her seat, looking as tense as I feel. Jessie gets to her feet to cheer for me, saying, "You can do it, Cory."

Throw a wild pitch, something inside my brain tells me. The bad thought happens all at once and is too much for me to tune out.

Throw a wild pitch.

Throw a wild pitch.

I take a few deep breaths. I focus on the red seam of the baseball.

As I get ready again, the noise from the other team is so loud I can't even hear what they're saying. But I know what they're doing, and I've had enough. I can feel the change in my mood, and the change in my body.

Instead of making me more nervous, their jeering is making me angry.

Throw a fastball for a strike, I tell myself. *Right down the middle. Faster than you've ever thrown before.*

This time I hurry through the touching so quickly

that I leave out a step, and when I let go of the ball, it flies straight and fast. The batter barely gets around and fouls it off for strike two.

Three balls, two strikes, I say to myself. *Now I have a chance.* And then the significance of what's just happened dawns on me: *I can still throw a good pitch even when they're yelling.*

"Show 'em, Cory. You can do it," Jessie calls out. "C'mon, Cory."

"You got 'em now," somebody else shouts.

"Right down the middle, baby."

"One more, just one more," my father calls out. "Go, Cory! You've got 'em!"

I have goose bumps all over my body. People are actually cheering for me.

I touch my nose once, but this time that's where the urge ends. My arms come to rest on my stomach.

The runners set themselves, ready for anything.

People on both sides of the field are standing and shouting.

Something inside me has changed and gotten really calm. I'm out here in a place I love, with the wind on my face, playing my favorite game in the world. This is tense, but I've been through a lot worse and come out alive. I can survive this, too.

I force my attention completely on the catcher's

mitt. Two seconds later I reach back with the ball, then let it go with more power than I've ever had before. The ball flies so straight and so fast I can hardly see it. Even before it gets there, I know that nothing can touch it.

And nothing does.

"Strike three. You're out!" the umpire yells at the batter.

The inning is over.

God, I love baseball.

Chapter 22

IF THIS HAD BEEN THE END of the most perfect afternoon in my life, it would have been more than enough to make me deliriously happy. But right now our team is still losing by two runs, and it's our final at bat.

I'm at the plate with two outs, and a new set of bending and twisting tics has set in. I look at the two guys on base and don't want to let them down.

Maybe it's the lesson I learned on the mound about not letting anything bother me, but when I see the ball coming in, I have only one point of focus.

When I swing, I feel solid impact on the fat part of

the bat. As the runners take off, the ball sails high in the air. It keeps going farther than any other ball has gone at this field, right over the center-field fence and into the parking lot. *I just hit a home run!*

When I get to home plate and break free from my teammates, I run to my family at the chain-link fence. Our fingers touch through the mesh, and they tell me that I'm great.

My God, I did something great, I think to myself.

A short time later, a friend of our family taps me on the shoulder. "I got this in the parking lot," he says, "so you never forget."

I take the home-run ball with a happy grin and thank him.

It's been years, and I still have the ball. I will always remember that special day, maybe the best day of my youth.

No, not maybe. It was.

Chapter 23

THE GOOD DAYS ARE FEW and far between, and maybe that's why I remember them so vividly.

It's late on a Sunday afternoon in the summer before seventh grade. My father and I are in a race against the sun somewhere in the mountains of north-eastern Pennsylvania. We've been looking for a lake called Wallenpaupack, but after what is supposed to be a two-hour drive turns into a three-and-a-half-hour drive, we're about to give up.

The tension in the car is like electricity flowing all around us. Out of anxiousness, I start to touch the steering wheel again, even though we're going fast.

My father doesn't mention it at first, but the next time I reach for the wheel, he can't stop himself.

"You can't do that, Cory. Do something else," he says, suddenly very annoyed.

Even though I realize that this urge seems dangerous to someone who's driving, I have an instant angry reaction to his warning. He knows it will only increase the urge. And he should understand by now that I would never again pull the wheel to one side, as I almost did with Mom right before our accident.

His outburst is especially surprising given that my father and I are getting along very well this summer. When I do something silly or dangerous such as grabbing at the steering wheel or shooting paintballs at our white garage doors, he knows how to handle it. He stays calm and asks me to think about the consequences of my actions, then walks away until I chill out.

My mother almost never gets upset with me, no matter what I do. She simply talks to me until I relax. I just wish she'd stop worrying so much. Sometimes I see a sadness in her eyes that makes me think my problems are never going to end and that they might even make her sick.

I move once more for the steering wheel, but this time I'm able to stop myself from touching it. Then the need goes away.

I still can't believe my father is taking this long road trip with me. He's doing it because he wants to spend some time together but also because I have nothing to do at home. My few friends have been going to the town pool and having parties and not inviting me, so my father has again taken over as my friend.

Chapter 24

THE SKY IS GETTING DIMMER. Ever since the idea of Jet Skiing came up, it's become a thrilling obsession for me. It's like riding a motorcycle full speed, only on the water. But we're obviously losing the race against time.

"I'm not sure we're going to make it," my father says. "It wasn't supposed to take this long. Sorry, Cory."

His words are like a knife sinking very deep into my stomach.

"We *have* to do it, Dad. Will you still try?"

He takes his eyes off the road to look at me. "I'm trying, Cory."

"It's okay," I surprise myself by saying. "It's okay if we can't do it. Thanks for trying, Dad."

My father's expression suddenly gets more determined.

"I didn't say we were giving up."

He sets his eyes back on the road and pushes down on the gas pedal.

A half hour later, it's getting more apparent that my dream isn't going to happen today. I'm making a chirping sound to get the tension out of my throat, and my right hand is shooting into the air over the dashboard.

Then a miracle. We see a road sign for a place called Hawley. My heart pounds in my chest. That's the name of a town near the lake.

"We have a chance," my father says with new energy, "but they said they only stay open until no one wants to ride."

That's a possibility I don't even want to think about.

Lake Wallenpaupack appears at the end of the road like magic. It's an endless body of water that looks like motor oil in the dimming light. The evergreen trees on a distant shoreline seem about a thousand miles away.

Two college-age boys in swimsuits are on the dock,

one sitting, the other tying up the last of six or seven Jet Skis for the night. No one else is around. No one is on the lake. My heart is sinking faster than the setting sun.

"I know it's late, but I'd really appreciate it if you'd let us take a ride," my father says to the boy on the chair. "We've been driving for hours."

The two guys look at each other. Not happy.

"We're closing up for the night," the chair guy says. "We open at eight tomorrow. Where are you staying?"

"We have no place to stay." My father nods in my direction. "I promised my son we'd be able to ride. It's really important to us."

The tension in the air makes my body twitch. Maybe they notice, maybe not.

After a long silence, the boy in the chair gets up and trudges to a small shack on the dock that serves as the office. My father turns to me with his eyebrows raised, and we follow him.

"I'll need his ID," the boy tells my father.

This is an unexpected shock. Age matters, even at such a faraway place as this. With all the weight I've gained, I'm big for my age, but I still look too young for this.

"We left so fast we forgot to bring it. But don't worry about that. He's ridden dozens of times. On vacations."

"I could get in trouble."

"I'll take full responsibility. I'll sign a paper if you want."

The boy thinks about it for a time. "I'll need a hundred-dollar deposit. You've got a half hour."

Chapter 25

THIS IS HEAVEN for me.

My dad and I are out so far on the lake that I wonder if we can ever find our way back. We've definitely been going for more than a half hour. The sun has set, and the golden sky is the only thing lighting up the water. If we wait too much longer, we'll be riding in the dark.

I'm the one who has taken us out this far from shore; my father is just following me. I can tell he's nervous about being in such deep water. Even I have to admit this water is very weird. It feels alive with things moving and wriggling under the surface like huge fish. The strangest thing is that although there are strong waves, there's no wind at all.

The surface swells have valleys in between that sometimes take us out of sight of each other until we rise again. When I get caught halfway up the side of a swell, it feels like the Jet Ski is going to tip over.

My father must be feeling it worse than I am. He keeps staring at the sky and his watch—although when I look back at him, he waves at me as if he's happy to be here.

Soon the sky is so dark that even I can feel a sense of danger approaching. My father motions to me, and I drive over to where he is. The water has now become almost motionless. We gently bob up and down with the sides of our skis touching.

"We have to go back now."

I nod in agreement.

The current catches hold of our Jet Skis for a moment. It gently turns us side by side until we're both looking out into the horizon, now only a thin slice of orange through the trees. In the stillness of a world that belongs only to us, I feel endlessly grateful toward my father. I don't know any other fathers who would have done so much to make this dream happen, or put up with me day after day.

"Thanks for doing this, Dad."

"I love you, Cory."

Then we slowly head back.

Chapter 26

OF COURSE, for every good time, another bad one isn't far off. That seems to be Cory's Law or something.

We're driving to one of the best hospitals in the country for people who can't control their body movements. Suddenly I don't feel so alone.

I can't believe there's an entire hospital for people whose bodies move in unusual ways. I wonder what the other patients are like, and if there is anyone there who does stranger things than I do. I doubt it very much.

I'm coming here because in recent months middle

school has become overwhelming, and I've started missing whole days at a time. I've even stopped playing baseball.

Risperdal has become my doctor's main weapon in the battle against my mind. It's calming me down and has stopped a lot of my wild behavior, but I'm paying a price.

At one and a half pills, I developed a new tic of head twisting and foot tapping in sequence. My weight had already gone up about forty pounds.

At two and a half pills, the foot thing stopped, but my tics became wilder and more unpredictable than ever.

Then came three pills. And four.

Suddenly I've become afraid of everything I used to like. I've always loved the ocean—the bigger the waves, the better. Lifeguards have had to order me out of the water after everyone else has left because of undertow or rip currents. With the increase in Risperdal, I've become afraid to go into even the calmest water. I've also started to suffer from vertigo and was so terrified of taking the ferry to Martha's Vineyard that I almost ruined our family vacation. I heard Dad saying to my mother that Risperdal took away my courage.

Still, in the hope that Risperdal would eventually

help, we got up to six pills a day, a dose that would make most people catatonic. One time my father accidentally took a single pill thinking it was something else, and he slept almost all day.

The high dose calmed me down enough to stop me from bouncing off the walls, but I began to shake my head so hard I was sure I'd damaged my brain. The increased dosage also shot me up to nearly 230 pounds, a lot for somebody who's five foot seven. I was afraid of doing anything that had the potential to hurt or scare me. And that's when enough became enough.

The decision to start taking me *off* Risperdal was harder than the one to put me on it. Internet chat rooms are full of horror stories about the physical pain of withdrawal from this drug, even when it's taken away a little at a time. And the accounts are all true. There were days when I screamed, and cried, and just wanted to die. My depression deepened, and I began to believe that the only purpose of my life was to be in pain.

Given how bad the withdrawal was and the fact that Risperdal had at least helped my behavior, I *had* to start back on some of it again. We also tried it in combination with old and new drugs such as Orap—which made me totally wild—and Zoloft and Klonopin. So many that I can't remember them all. And nothing helped.

During this period, out of desperation, my parents found a chiropractor two hours away in Connecticut who said he could help my movement disorder by snapping a part of my upper spine. My father was worried about that and asked the chiropractor to demonstrate it on him. It was such a violent snap that my father said he actually saw stars, and he decided it was too risky for me.

After that, we found an unusual environmental allergist in the southern part of our state. He believed that my problems were caused by ingesting the wrong foods or chemicals, and that if he could figure out what they were, he could fix me. He may have been right, but I'll never know. He wanted me to go on a diet that was too strict to even try. With Risperdal making me hungry all the time, and with eating now an obsession, the thought of losing my favorite foods was unbearable.

The most extreme thing we almost tried came up while we were on vacation in Florida. A social worker by the pool noticed my movements and introduced herself. She said that I should try *swimming with dolphins* because they had healing powers that could take away my Tourette's. It sounded crazy, but she seemed pretty smart. My mother tried to set it up, but all the time slots were filled. Otherwise I would have gone for the swimming-with-dolphins treatment.

Which explains why I'm here today, turning onto the side street that leads to the Stringer Clinic for Neurological Movement Disorders.

It sure sounds like my kind of place.

Chapter 27

AS MY PARENTS and I travel up the elevator to the third floor to see the doctors, my tics get the message and shift into high gear. The doors open onto a long, narrow waiting area with a single wooden bench that runs along one wall.

It's before nine a.m., so the glass door that leads to the inner office is still locked. We're always early for these appointments. I guess that's because we're always so hopeful.

We sit and wait in silence. My father is thumbing through old magazines; my mother is trying to look optimistic, as usual planning to spend her whole day

119

with me. Since my head started shaking all those years ago, she's given up her own business, writing, and any thought of a career.

The next time the elevator arrives at our floor, a teenage boy comes out with a condition no one would believe unless they saw it for themselves. My first thought is that he must have dropped something and is trying to pick it up.

But as he leaves the elevator, he doesn't stand. Instead, he moves forward like an animal. He places both hands ahead of his body on the ground and keeps them there until his legs catch up. This allows him to take another stride. Amazing as it seems, this must be how he moves all the time and why he's here. This is his movement disorder, as big an understatement as there has ever been.

After three steps, he jumps up on the bench and swings his legs around to face forward. He does this so effortlessly it's clear he must have done it a thousand times.

Once he's settled on the bench, he looks straight ahead without checking our reactions. That's something I totally understand. I've learned how *not* to see people staring at me, too.

Not wanting to embarrass him, I study him out of the corner of my eye. Sitting, he appears to be completely calm and normal. He's older than I am by five or six years, which would make him about eighteen. He's good-looking, with intelligent eyes.

His mother is showing a lot of self-control, too. My heart goes out to both of them. I can't imagine what it's like to get up every morning knowing that some power you can't control will force you to move around like a gorilla. All he probably wants to do is just stand up straight. How cheated he must feel, how he must hurt inside. I wonder if he ever runs into anyone worse off than himself, like I just have. I don't think I could survive what he has, but I guess I'd find a way.

I've thought about what a place that treats movement disorders would look like. I pictured the laboratory in *Frankenstein*. In reality, the building is like a large city hospital, all cement and windows. The closest parking is a few blocks away, so by the time I hopped, skipped, and jumped to the front door, I was tired out, and the day hadn't even started yet.

My mother has told me that the Stringer Clinic is one of the best hospitals in the world for research into unusual body movements, especially Parkinson's disease. Since I'm beginning to believe that any cure for what I have will eventually have to come from me, I'm mainly here to please my parents.

Our appointment with the well-known Dr. Holmes

has been a great accomplishment for my mother. At first they told Mom that the doctor was too busy to see me, but when Mom described how severe my movements were and started to cry, they agreed to make room in the doctor's busy day.

This is a truly depressing thought. Being able to attract the attention of someone this famous only clues me in to how extreme my case must be.

Chapter 28

DR. HOLMES SEEMS TO BE involved more in research than in the actual treatment of patients. Her biography on the Internet is very impressive.

In a short time, I'll wish that I'd never heard of her or her hospital. I'm about to learn the meaning of the phrase *living hell*.

In theory the hospital's advanced research and treatments for Parkinson's disease are important for me because that illness also causes involuntary movements. Like Tourette's, Parkinson's has something to do with two chemicals the brain produces, dopamine and serotonin. We've been told that Dr. Holmes has had great success treating Tourette's patients, too.

When we're finally admitted inside, we're directed to a larger waiting room that before long fills up with other patients. There are many doctors working in this area of the hospital.

There seems to be a special bond among patients in places like this because everyone has the same kinds of problems. Most of the patients here are older, and a few have come with family members.

The man who takes a seat next to us is probably in his seventies and doesn't look well. He's bent over and his skin is pasty white, like pie dough. Soon he strikes up a conversation with my mother. He's a doctor himself, researching treatments for Parkinson's disease, which he suffers from. In his case, the sickness has progressed to its later stages. He has only a short time left, he admits as a matter of fact, and wants to survive long enough to finish his research, which could help with a possible cure for Parkinson's. He says that Dr. Holmes is the best in this field, and he hopes she can give him a few extra months to finish his work.

When his name is called, he turns to me with eyes that have seen a lot of suffering and says, "Good luck to you." I know I'll never see him again, and it makes me feel sad.

Chapter 29

DR. HOLMES'S ASSISTANT is a young, soft-spoken but very intense man who takes my medical history. He spends most of the time on my past medicines and their exact doses.

My mother has brought her precise daily notes on my meds and their effects on me, which she has kept since the beginning.

A door I hadn't noticed opens, and Dr. Holmes enters, surrounded by three other doctors in long white coats who look more like scientists. Two of them have clipboards, and no one speaks but Holmes, a tall and strict-looking woman with round glasses, maybe in her mid-fifties. She ignores me completely at first, choosing to skim over the notes her assistant has taken. When she's done, she looks up at me without even so much as a smile. She's all business.

"What are your present symptoms?" she asks as though she's dealing with a grown-up patient.

I don't know where to start. "I do a lot of things," I tell her, scrunching up my face. "Twist my neck, make sounds…different things at different times. Right now I'm hopping a lot."

For some reason, the hopping gets her attention.

"Would you show me?"

I'm surprised and uncomfortable at this request. No doctor has ever asked me to perform my tics, maybe because they are so obvious, they don't have to. With all these new doctors staring at me, my eyes are twitching continuously, and when I stand, my body bends at the waist and I bob up and down a few times as if I'm doing a warm-up exercise. I haven't done this one in a while.

Dr. Holmes directs me to walk to the end of the hall, a distance of about thirty feet. Almost immediately, my legs get a freeze-up feeling, and I have to take a few hops to relieve the tension.

Three or four quick hops in place, some more walking, then three or four more.

The first set of hops is mild compared to the second, which almost trips me up. When I look back to check Dr. Holmes's reaction, I notice that one of her assistants has been videotaping me. Suddenly I'm embarrassed and angry. No one has asked if they could take my picture. I don't know who they're going to show this to.

The general feeling I've had since I came into this office is that *I'm not a person; I'm a specimen on display.*

I turn back to the far wall and try not to think about it. I tell myself that they've seen so many other lab rats they've forgotten rats have feelings, too.

It's another fifteen feet to the end of the corridor, and because I'm extra tense, I hop every few steps until I get there. At the end of the last jump, I lose my balance and fall forward. Only my outstretched hands stop me from crashing into the wall, maybe smashing a few teeth.

After the videotaping, the men in the white coats leave and I go back to my chair with several more hops, none as extreme as the one that almost made me fall.

"We understand that you've treated Tourette's cases," my father says to Dr. Holmes, getting right to it, as usual.

"Yes, a large number of them," she answers.

"How many have you helped...I mean...well, as a percentage?" my father asks, trying to pin Holmes down. He's as suspicious as I am and is never afraid to be direct.

"About eighty percent," Holmes says without hesitation.

None of us is expecting a number that exact or that high. It's too good to believe, even though I want to. The last thing I need is another false hope, but it means a lot when a woman of her stature makes such a specific claim. She's instantly put a chink in my armor.

"From what I've seen so far, I'm fairly certain my treatment will work for your son," she adds without much emotion, as if this life-changing, lifesaving promise is everyday small talk. She's all about facts and research.

"The treatment is simple," she goes on to say. "We use tetrabenazine. Most of our patients respond well to it. The dosage has to be monitored closely, however."

My rising hopes are suddenly smashed. After all the buildup, Dr. Holmes is only talking about another medicine. One more to add to the long list.

In a few minutes, the meeting ends abruptly when the doctor just gets up and walks out of the room, cutting off any more discussion. Not even a good-bye.

After another meeting with Dr. Holmes's assistant,

we stop off at a reception desk and are given a form to sign that lets us get the tetrabenazine, which, it turns out, isn't usually legal to prescribe in the United States, except through a few special licenses, one of which Dr. Holmes has.

During the ride home we all sit in silence. Even with the name of yet another drug ringing in our ears, there is an air of subdued excitement, as there has been every single time we've gotten a new medicine or a new piece of advice. A faint ray of hope. Not much of one, as far as I'm concerned, but better than nothing.

Or maybe not.

Chapter 30

IT TAKES more than a week to get tetrabenazine, or TBZ, because we have to get it from Canada. Dr. Holmes made me think that it was an experimental drug, but a Web site I check says it's been used in countries outside the United States since 1960.

It turns out it's an antipsychotic created to treat schizophrenia, just like Risperdal.

Here we go again.

Mom calls Dr. Pressler to check on her experience with TBZ but gets her answering machine. By now, Dr. Pressler has moved too far away for us to see her in person, but she's always there, returning our calls quickly, sharing results of medicines she's prescribed for her thousands of Tourette's patients, and telling us about new medicines.

The first night, I take my prescribed dose and fall asleep with an uncomfortable new feeling. My body is restless almost immediately, and I toss and turn continuously to find more comfortable positions. My tics are worse, too, but the high level of agitation is the bigger problem.

The next day, after we report my symptoms to Dr. Holmes's assistant, he tells us to *raise* the dose.

That night, the restless feeling increases so much that my whole body starts bouncing around the bed, kind of like the girl in *The Exorcist.* As the agitation gets worse, I plead with my mother to make it go away. She tells me to try to wait it out, and I curse at her because she won't help me. *I curse at my mother?* There's another person inside of me, taking over.

She gives me a second dose of Benadryl to help me sleep, but two hours later I'm still jerking and twisting and bouncing up and down. I'm exhausted from the meds, but it feels like there are a thousand fire ants in my bloodstream. I want to jump out of my skin.

Another hour passes, and it seems like forever. I take a third dose of Benadryl and some extra Risperdal. Between the heavy sedation and all the energy I've used, I gratefully pass out at around three thirty.

As strong as I usually am, I don't think I can take much more of this.

I am officially in hell.

Chapter 31

THE NEXT MORNING, Dr. Holmes's assistant casually tells us that my reaction is a well-known condition called *akathisia*. His advice is to wait it out until my body adjusts — otherwise we'll never know if TBZ is what we've been looking for. *How many times have I heard that about a new medicine?* As a possible solution, he orders another *increase* in the dosage, saying that this will help me adjust more quickly. I don't get why taking more of a bad thing can help, but he's the doctor. And this is his advice.

The following day, Dr. Pressler calls back and tells us that she hasn't prescribed tetrabenazine for me because it hasn't worked for any of her other patients. She's not sure of Dr. Holmes and her success in treating Tourette's syndrome with TBZ, but she says that since everyone's chemistry is different, there's always a chance it could help.

Over the next few days, the medicine takes me to another level. During the daytime, when it wears off a bit, my agitation changes into a heavily drugged feeling, as if I'm living in slow motion. I sit in place for long periods, my eyes glazed over and my mouth hanging open. I actually drool.

I don't know where I am in time and space, and I'm so limp that some of my tics go away. But something really bad is happening with my worst leg tic.

As I get up from my computer, I hop in place as I have before, but this time I hop on my heels. This makes it easy to lose my balance, and I fall backward, crashing into the French doors behind me and hitting my head on the floor.

My parents come running at the noise and find me unhurt. But I just lie there with no idea of what happened. I have a silly, embarrassed smile on my face because I feel so stoned. In my hazy state, I tell them I'm all right and apologize for falling. They help me up, but as soon as I'm standing, I hop and fall backward again. This time my father catches me before I hit the ground.

The doctor at the Stringer Clinic has the same answer to this as he had before: we have to stay with the program. We've gone too far to give up on TBZ. Unbelievably, he hikes the dose of the medicine again.

That night the akathisia goes beyond my ability to handle it. I writhe in bed, literally trying to scratch my skin off, screaming for my mother to please kill me. I can't wear any clothes because they hurt my skin. I beg for more and more Benadryl, but even that doesn't help until doses of other drugs I'm taking are added.

The daytime pattern continues, especially the feeling of being in the ozone layer. I go through the motions of living, moving slowly from place to place, trying to respond to things happening around me. But I'm in a total zombie daze. It's like watching the world from a thousand miles away, from another level of reality, from someone else's body.

One afternoon my father takes me to my favorite Chinese restaurant, and when the waiter places my meal in front of me, I just stare ahead with a long string of drool hanging down from my mouth. I imagine I'll never forget the sad look on my father's face as he watches me try to eat, to function on the most basic level.

I'm not living the life everyone else is living. I'm not here anymore.

That night I'm like one of those screaming patients you see in old movies, the ones getting electroshock therapy in insane asylums. I tell my mother I want to die, I want her to kill me, and she's frantic. Somehow I get through the night with more drugs.

When we report in to the doctors at Stringer, they finally agree that the treatment isn't working. The tetrabenazine is decreased gradually so I don't have more dangerous side effects.

In a day or two, the akathisia begins to go away, too. My vision clears, and slowly I become part of the world again. *And my tics go right back to where they were.*

Dr. Pressler isn't surprised that the medicine hasn't helped, but she is surprised to learn how high the doses were, even the first, which is probably why my body reacted so badly.

"Falling over backward is a classic symptom of overdose from drugs used to treat Parkinson's disease," she tells us.

The worst part is that there may have been no need for the painful hours I spent with akathisia.

"It could have been stopped quickly with Cogentin," she says. "It's a well-known antidote for Parkinson's patients who overdose on tetrabenazine."

Dr. Pressler has no idea why our new doctors didn't tell us that. Her reaction makes me wonder whether they let my trial go on longer than it should have because they really believed it would work or because they were actually using me for research.

Whatever the answer, I was in a dangerous place because of this drug. When the akathisia was at its worst, I wasn't in my right mind. I wanted to kill myself. If you had handed me a gun, I would have used it.

When it was all over, I was consumed by obsessive thoughts of getting even with the famous doctor and her hospital for what they put me through. I wanted to go back and tell them what they did to me, and to sue them and give the proceeds to the Tourette Syndrome Association. Of course, I had no idea if their actions justified a lawsuit. I just wanted to do something.

Yet, in the end, our family didn't do anything. That's the problem with having a condition as hard to treat as mine: there are only a few doctors who have a chance to help, so you can't make them angry or burn bridges no matter what they do to you.

And that's why when I talk about the famous Dr. Holmes, I don't use her real name. As bad as her advice turned out to be, I never know when I might have to go back to her with another desperate cry for help.

Holding On, but Just Barely

Chapter 32

I CAN TELL by how quietly my mother and father are talking downstairs that they don't want me to hear them, so they're probably discussing me. They're doing this more and more lately, especially after a bad day like today.

This afternoon I noticed my mother lying down next to our golden retriever, River. Mom's head was pressed tightly into the dog's chest, and she stayed that way for a long time. River always seems to understand what's going on in our family. Once, when he heard my mother crying, he started to howl softly with her.

Today when my father walked in the door, Mom told him what had happened at school. He often comes home from long workdays to bad news about me.

I had seriously disturbed the class again, and one of the other parents had called the teacher to complain. My mother had to go to a conference after school to talk about what to do with me. My father got mad when he heard about it. He gets angry at the people who make things harder for me. I hope he's not mad at me now.

Sometimes I think my problems will get to be too much for my mother and father to take, and that maybe they'll become so unhappy they won't stay together. I know this can happen, because it did to a few of my friends' parents who didn't have nearly as many problems as we do.

I'm also worried that Jessie doesn't love me as much as she used to. She complains to my parents all the time now that they pay more attention to me than to her, especially when she's having a hard time. Today Jessie's best friend ditched her for no reason at all, and when she came home, she had to hear about my bad day before she could tell them about hers.

I think Jessie is having a harder time with me now

than when we were younger because she has conflicting feelings about me. She still wants to protect me from anyone who makes fun of me, and a lot of times she tells off kids who are bigger than she is. But she's also mad at me because I make it difficult for her to have friends and a normal life. I guess that's what a lot of our fights are really about. It must be hard loving a brother who makes your life worse. Even so, most of the time she's great to me.

I'm still awake, and after my parents have talked for a long time, I get worried and tiptoe down the stairs.

At the landing, I peek around the banister and see my father standing with his back to me. He has his arms around my mother, and he's hugging her tight, and it makes me feel so good and warm to see them that way.

Then, when he lets her go, I can she that she's been crying. She wipes her eyes when she sees me and tries to make her face look like it's smiling, but it isn't. She takes me back to bed, saying there's nothing to worry about. Mom tells me a joke and kisses me on the forehead, and I feel okay again.

One good thing, I guess, is that all of us have been living this kind of life for a long time. Even though bad things happen, we get over them somehow. We laugh and we cry and we fight and then we make up and tell one another *I love you*. A lot of *sorry*s and hugging and kissing and chasing River around the dining room table.

That's my family.

Chapter 33

I'VE BEEN IN FRONT OF my computer for more than twenty hours now and I'm not even getting tired. I've studied courses on Internet marketing for up to a day and a half straight. Being compulsive has its advantages—sometimes, anyway.

Tonight, though, there's something new building inside of me. It's a feeling I've had before, but now it's stronger and wants to bust loose. It's like knowing you're going to be sick and throw up: it's just a matter of *when*.

It's hard to believe, but I'm actually getting through middle school, even though I'm missing a lot of classes.

This is mainly because of homeschooling and my ability to remember just about everything I hear in class.

The torture of tetrabenazine has finally worn off, but different parts of my body are still cutting loose at any given moment. At this point there's a huge list of drugs that are in my bloodstream.

BuSpar to sedate me, and Tenex, another high-blood-pressure drug. And higher doses of Risperdal again because I'm worse when I'm off it than when I'm on it, and getting off it completely is terrible.

But being out of control for so many years—and what that's done to my life—is pushing me to a place I don't want to go.

A needed break from the computer comes when Jamie shows up at my front door around eight o'clock. I'm grateful for the company, even though he and I hardly ever spend time together. Jamie drifts in and out of the small group of people whom I've started to hang out with in my basement.

Each of them is strange in his own way, but I think Jamie is the weirdest of all. He almost never smiles, his face rarely shows what he's thinking, and he's very moody.

I give Jamie a big welcome, like he's my best friend in the world, but as usual he doesn't react. Jamie and

I have a strange relationship. Sometimes he seems like a true friend, but then something happens and he flips out, and I don't hear from him for weeks at a time.

For a while we play video games on my computer and fool around with a hacking program that fascinates both of us.

Everything goes okay until I have the need to touch Jamie's shoulder three times in a row. I haven't had this strange urge in a long time and thought it was gone. I try not to do it but can't fight off the feeling.

Finally I touch him as lightly as I can, but he cringes away from me like I have a contagious disease, and he orders me not to do it again.

I think his reaction is way out of proportion to what I did. Jamie is aware of my *have-to-touch* tic. Everyone knows that it doesn't mean anything, but Jamie has his own problems. I think he takes medicine for something, but he doesn't talk about it. He's one kid you never want to touch, *which is probably why I did it.*

Since a single series of touches hasn't completed my have-to-touch routine, a little while later I tap him.

Now Jamie freaks out. He jumps up from his chair and curses me, then storms out of the house so fast I can only sit there in amazement. I can't believe how quickly a good time has turned bad again, how my tics have ruined another night. My body is always betraying me, *always, always, always.*

This sudden ditching by Jamie causes something else to happen. The feeling that was with me earlier at the computer is growing stronger. It's bigger and badder than before, and it's taking on its own life. I feel it surging inside — like a giant wave that wants to break powerfully on the shore.

I get up and try to walk it off, but there's something urgent about this. I feel like I'm getting sick to my stomach, but it has nothing to do with vomiting.

And then, right in the middle of a hopping tic, the tsunami hits full force.

Chapter **34**

THE ALMOST COMPLETE LOSS OF CONTROL happens all at once. The wave inside breaks and forces me to cry out with such raw fury that my throat feels like it was sandpapered.

I want to move, to outrun whatever is going on inside me, but a stabbing pain in my belly makes me go down. I hit the floor as though I've been punched by a weight lifter or a heavyweight boxer.

By the time my parents hear me raging, I'm unable to control it any more than I can control my tics. My anger is wild fury, and suddenly it's directed at them.

I'm scaring myself because I've never felt anything like this before.

I curse my father when he tries to calm me, and I make a threatening move at him when he gets too close. I blame him for my suffering. I'm ultraviolent and want to strike out at anything and everything around me.

Before long I'm in another world, this one not even close to rational.

I can feel the skin around my mouth pucker and tighten. My eyes have narrowed and made the world darker. My lips are pulled back like a snarling wolf's. I feel my brain unraveling, detaching from any normal thought process.

I'm unreachable, even to myself.

I shout that I can't take it anymore and bolt for the living room, where I fall to the floor with a loud groan, clutching my stomach again. I thrash around, then dry heave. It seems the only question is, which will burst first, my brain or my heart?

In a while the rage is still there, and I'm getting desperate. I pull myself up and head to the kitchen to take medicine so I can put myself out as fast as possible.

I go crazy and take all my medicines at once: trazodone to wipe me out; propranolol and Xanax for my anxiety.

I add two Benadryl, almost choking on the slippery pills. When I'm finished, dozens of pills are all over the floor.

Waiting for the medicines to work, I give up fighting and collapse onto the ground again, wondering where this insanity will take me and if I'll ever get back. My parents are trying to help me—something they've done since I was four—but there's nothing they can do, nothing anyone can do.

I finally yell at them to leave me alone, to get away from me. They're petrified and do as I say. That's good, because I'm afraid I could hurt them right now.

I latch the kitchen door.

A red-hot pain in my stomach explodes with such intensity that I double over in agony. The loudest scream I have ever made almost bursts my throat. It's a torrent of pent-up rage spewing out, a lava flow of all the years of pain, embarrassment, insults and ridicule, tics and bad thoughts, betrayal by friends, and helplessness—all of it, plus the fiery ball still glowing in my belly, trying to burn its way outside.

Once let loose, the full rage takes control of me. From the kitchen floor, I grab the bottom of a stool and crash it against two others, splintering one of the legs.

I pull myself up to the countertop and bring my

fist down on a glass fruit bowl, breaking it into pieces. Then I violently sweep everything else on the counter onto the floor and kick it out of my way.

I see the drawer with the knives in it and wonder what it would be like to end it this way. I can't stop thinking about hurting myself. I open the drawer and grab one of the big jagged-edged knives.

I hold it in front of my eyes, fascinated with the idea of dying. My hand is shaking uncontrollably.

I hold the knife to my throat and feel a tingle at being so close to cutting myself, a mixture of excitement and dread. *Maybe I'm going to do it. Maybe I'll have to do it.* It's like being on the edge of a cliff or standing on the balcony of a tall building and just for a moment thinking there's something inside you that's going to make you jump. I feel totally crazy, capable of anything.

My parents are talking to me through the kitchen door, trying to calm me down. They have no idea how bad this is, though. *They're not me.*

At the last moment, I pull the knife away from my body. I throw it with all my might at the wall near the kitchen table. I miss, and it sails over the table and breaks through the double kitchen window behind it.

I spin around to the refrigerator, remembering the

bottle of vodka my parents keep in the freezer. I nearly tear the door off getting to it, then put the bottle to my mouth and take six or seven big gulps.

My legs finally give out, and I'm back on the floor, waiting for numbness to set in. Eventually, it gets dark.

Sometime later, I'm still lying there, now with a pillow under my head.

The lights are turned down and I've been sleeping. The rage is gone, replaced by warmth, as though I'm sitting near a fireplace. The burning in my stomach has stopped. My heartbeat is slow and regular. I listen to my own breathing in the silence of the house and feel like I'm alone in heaven after rising out of hell.

I had thought that this life couldn't get any worse, but I was wrong.

"Cory?" I hear a whisper.

Chapter 35

MY MOTHER is standing over me. She kneels and asks if there's anything she can do to help, and I just stare at her. I've come back from a nightmare world that neither of us has ever known, and there aren't words to make her understand where I've been.

The only thing I know for sure is that the raging person I was a few hours ago isn't me now. I'm back. *This is Cory, not that other crazy guy.*

I feel shame and remorse and don't know where to start. "Sorry. Sorry, Mom" is all I can think to say.

"I know," she whispers. "Me, too."

She reaches down to pull me up, but the drugs and alcohol have left me without strength, and I can't help her.

She puts her arms around me and, as big as I am, somehow hoists me to my feet and holds me. My father is behind her now, and he takes my hand. This would make *some* family portrait, I guess. Not exactly Norman Rockwell.

We stand that way for a long time, breathing in the same exact rhythm, our bellies going in and out against one another's.

In time they get me up the stairs and put me in bed. I try to remember what happened, but I can't force myself to think about it anymore.

I have one last thought as I drift off to sleep.

Whatever it was that took over will be back. Soon. I just know it.

The next day, I go to the computer and write a letter to my mother and father and place it on the kitchen counter.

Dear Mom and Dad,
   I feel so bad for what happened last night. Every time I think about it, my actions seem more and more ridiculous. I can't believe I

cursed at both of you like that. I know it wasn't me, because I would never ever blow up at you when you were only trying to help.

Mom, the fact that I made you cry makes me want to shoot myself. Out of all the things in life, seeing you cry absolutely kills me. I feel like a beast. It's like I took the most loving angel and broke its heart over nothing. Mom, you are an angel to me. I'm the luckiest kid in the world to have you as my mom. I would take Tourette's one hundred times as bad and be condemned to a wheelchair for my whole life, unable to move my body, just so I could have you as my mother. I really mean it. I love you, Mom, and I'm very sorry for hurting you.

Dad, I also feel terrible for raging at you. I know all you want to do is help me and make me happy. And I love you more than you can imagine. And I know you don't deserve one bit of it. You're the best dad I could have ever asked for, and I'm incredibly lucky to have you as my dad.

Even though I've got a harder life than many other people, you guys totally turned the tables on what could have been a tough life and turned it into a blessed life, full of love, caring, and happiness. You're more than I could have ever asked for or imagined. I love you both so much and hope you'll accept my apologies. I love you, Mom and Dad.

Cory

Part Three

FALLING DOWN, PICKING MYSELF UP

Chapter 36

"THE NEXT MEDICINE will be the one that works."

"Your body will calm down as you get older."

"If you can just hold on until middle school, things will get better."

"If you can just hold on until high school, things will get better."

These are the promises that help keep me going. And in my mind, the summer before high school is going to be the time that the bell will ring and everything will change.

Except it doesn't happen.

159

That summer comes at me one day and one event at a time, and there is no triumphant arrival into a more normal world.

Around the beginning of August, when everyone is bored and looking for something to do, a neighborhood girl invites me to come hang out at her house. While I am there, her brother and his buddies take the bike I leave on her porch.

Another "friend" steals a paintball gun of mine, and someone takes my cell phone and rings up more than five hundred dollars in long-distance charges. And these are the kids I am closest to.

On most nights I go to the Burger King parking lot, where those of us with nothing better to do end up. Somebody gets booze, and we head for the local park, where we lie on the grass and drink. The police constantly harass us. It is the best I can do for a social life. Of course, I hide all this from my parents.

Chapter 37

I FINALLY ENTER high school, and the biggest surprise is that nothing has really changed. It's turning out to be as much of a minefield as middle school. Instead of becoming nicer as they've grown up, some of the meanest kids have become smarter at using my weaknesses for fun and games. It's as important as ever for them to look cool, and they do it by putting down others who are different or have problems. I'm an easy target, and it makes me feel bad just about every single day of high school.

This Friday morning is freezing cold. Another reason—besides the medicine-and-booze cocktail that's still working in my system from last night—to stay in bed. If I let them, the Xanax and Risperdal would keep me asleep for half the day. And maybe that's not the worst thing, actually. Sleeping is the one time I don't have to think.

When I finally do get out of bed, I hop.

This morning I stomp down so hard on the old wooden planks of my floor that a booming sound shakes the whole house. After years of taking my punishing blows, many of the planks have split open. The ceiling of the room under mine has cracks in it from the vibrations. Floor tiles in my shower are shattered for the same reason. *Welcome to my space.*

Not all of the damage is from my feet. My bedroom door is split down the middle from another violent rage attack during the summer. My raging is also the reason for the holes in the walls around the house. I could keep a carpenter busy full-time.

In my bathroom the scale says 243 pounds, a new high. At five foot eight, I'm getting more and more obese from Risperdal, my late-night feeding frenzies, and an ever-increasing number of liquor binges. Alcohol is better for giving my body and mind some blessed peace than any medicine I've ever taken.

"Breakfast is ready," my mother calls at nine o'clock.

It's another shortened high school day for me, since I'm not able to go to all eight periods.

Downstairs, I walk through the kitchen without stopping. "Got to have a cigarette first," I tell my mother, heading for the outdoor deck.

"Can't you wait? At least put something on!" she shouts after me. My mom hates that I smoke, but she also knows she has to pick her fights with me.

Outside, the temperature is cold enough for me to see my breath. I sit in a metal chair, puffing away, not caring that all I have on is a short-sleeve T-shirt. My craving for nicotine has become so strong that I can't get through an hour without a smoke. I'm also obsessing over my need for cigarettes, which makes my craving worse than that of most smokers, because it's not just about the nicotine.

My father has a business meeting in the area today, so he's able to drive me to school. On the way, I need music to calm me down, but a new compulsion makes me turn the volume to the highest level *before* turning on the radio. The sudden explosion of sound makes my father almost drive off the road.

"Jesus, Cory!"

"Sorry. Sorry."

The second time I hit the volume control turns out to be the last . . . for this trip, anyway.

There's a hole in the dashboard where the cigarette

lighter used to be. My father is one step ahead of me here. The last time we drove together, I got the lighter red-hot and then just barely touched it to my nose until I almost burned myself. I had to get into the backseat to stop doing it.

"Hope you have a better day," he tells me as I get out of the car.

"I will. I feel pretty good. Thanks for the ride."

Before I get to the front door at school, I do my leg shuffle, followed by a brand-new tic that seems to have developed just for the occasion. Every few seconds, I punch the air three times in a row, then bring my fist to my chest for a beat, then punch again. I do this one or two more times before getting to the door. What a way to start.

The days go on pretty much like this, and little by little I'm getting through my classes. Each day has good and bad moments. My teachers mostly like me and call on me whenever they can, and my life has as much structure as I can expect.

And then, something amazing happens, and things actually start to get better. It's the last thing anyone expects, maybe the most unlikely event in the history of the world, at least from my point of view.

I join the high school football team.

Chapter 38

IT'S A COLD, windy October Saturday at our high school football stadium. Our opponents are physically larger and from a much tougher town, but against all odds we're winning by a point and the game is almost over.

Now they're on our two-yard line, close to a score.

There are only a few seconds left on the clock, and everyone in the stands is holding their breath. The next play will decide the game.

By some miracle, not only am I playing football but I'm the second-fastest member of our team. The coach is using me on both offense and defense almost every play of the game.

But as good as I am, my tics are still part of the deal, and in the few seconds before the ball is snapped, my body is one of the only things moving on the field.

My main position is called noseguard. That means I'm on the defensive line opposite the other team's center. My job is to burst off the line the second the ball is snapped and try to tackle whoever gets the ball before the play can get going.

On the field, I feel like one of the luckiest people in the world. Nature has given me the strength and speed to get into the offensive backfield before my opponents know what hit them. And the weight I've gained on Risperdal is a good thing for football. I'm faster than anyone can believe for a guy as heavy as I am, and I don't let anything or anyone get in my way. Talk about a means for unloading your anger.

Because I was hyperexcited about today's big game, my mother gave me an extra Risperdal to calm me down. That makes six and a half pills, but they haven't taken away an ounce of my energy.

My mom, my dad, and Jessie are sitting in the stands at the fifty-yard line, cheering for me. I can always hear Jessie's voice because it's high-pitched and loud. I can't tell you what a huge day this is for our family, and for me, of course.

As the opposing quarterback calls his signals, I get into my three-point stance, my right hand balancing me on the ground.

I can feel this tremendous tension building in my legs. Suddenly, before the play starts, I make three rapid hops that take me into the neutral zone, considered a crime in high school football.

A horrified gasp rises from the crowd, but there are no penalty flags. Before the game, the referees were informed of my involuntary movements, and the league has made an exception for me.

The quarterback's count goes on longer than usual — he seems nervous, running through his audibles twice.

This gives my left arm time to spasm, and it shoots out into the sacred no-man's-land that separates the two teams. This movement has been startling the center opposite me all day. No matter how many times I've done it, he can't get used to the idea. He's pissed off when no flags are thrown.

I recover quickly from my arm thrust and plant my legs solidly on the ground. My body is like a stick of dynamite with a lit fuse.

When I hear the quarterback call *hike,* I ignite and

explode off the line into the center before the guy can even get upright. My sudden impact knocks him backward, and as he fights for balance, he grabs my leg with one hand. But I'm already halfway past him and tear loose from his grip.

The quarterback sees me coming and tries to dodge out of the way, but he's too late. I plant my helmet into his belly and lift him right off the ground. Both of us go crashing down, with everyone else piling on.

The refs' whistles blow just as a gun goes off, marking the end of the game. The home-team crowd, my crowd, is hysterical with joy. They've just witnessed a huge upset, in more ways than one—this was a game of me against my life, and this time, I won.

I feel my teammates' hands pulling me out of the pile of bodies and pounding me on the back. The crowd is standing and cheering wildly.

At first I can't hear what they are saying. Then I realize they are chanting my name.

"Cory! Cory! Cory!"

I'm embarrassed. I'm not used to being a hero. There's no other place in my life that this happens. Except in the old days, in Little League.

I head to the sidelines, hopping a few more times before I get there, and my coaches are actually hugging me. When I get a chance, I search the stands for my family. Dad's arm is wrapped around my mom, and he's beaming with pride and happiness. This is almost too much for me to stand, all this happiness and joy.

A short while later, the stadium is emptying out. As I walk to our car with my family, I can see how proud they all are of me. Jessie has been a star athlete in basketball, soccer, and lacrosse, but no one expected me to be back in sports after baseball ended. And they know that a day like this is about a lot more than football.

Now it's just the four of us. My teammates are leaving with one another in groups of two and three, joking and bragging and reliving the best game of the year so far.

Now and then as they pass by, a few of them congratulate me, but they don't stay around or invite me to come along.

Inside our car, I sit in silence with a curious mixture of emotions: a sense of pride but also an empty, achy feeling in the pit of my stomach. It's hard for me to understand how I can go from being a hero to being alone again, in just a couple of minutes.

"You're one of the best players they've ever had here. You're amazing, Cory, and they all know it," my mother says with a hand on my cheek.

"Yeah, I guess."

"I'm so proud of you, Cory," Dad says. "That was one of the best days of *my* life."

I don't let them know what I'm really feeling right now. Why should I, when it will only make them as sad as I am?

"Yeah," I say. "Me, too."

Chapter 39

A WEEK LATER, the football team is called together to meet a new coach. I'm not really sure what happened, whether it was school politics or not. The new guy is one of those really strict types with lots of rules such as *You smoke, you're off the team* and *Anyone late for practice doesn't play in the next game. No exceptions.*

These are two particularly tough rules for me, since I smoke like a chimney and, with my body problems, I'm always late getting anywhere.

A few days before the biggest game of our season, our practice is moved from the stadium to the weight room. Because I've gotten to school late, I don't know about the change until I get to the field and find it empty.

This makes me incredibly anxious because I know the new coach will be really pissed. My legs start to buckle under me, and the hopping spasms come one after another.

They get so bad that I can't stand up for very long, and by the time I arrive at the weight room, I am literally crawling to the door. It's never been this bad, not even close. But at least I'm finally here.

I manage to stumble into the weight room ten or fifteen minutes late, and the coach turns his anger on me in front of the rest of the guys.

"I told you I won't stand for anyone coming to practice late. That goes for you, too."

"I couldn't help it."

"I don't want to hear your lame excuses. You'll have to learn the hard way."

The rest of the guys don't like what's happening. Anyone can see that I'm covered in sweat, but no one says anything in my defense. They're too afraid of the coach. The practice session goes on without any further lectures, and I lift weights with everyone else. I figure everything is going to be all right. I hope so.

The next weekend, I'm suited up to play and mentally ready. It's an important game, and I know I can help the team. Right after the pregame pep talk, the new coach takes me aside.

"You're benched," he barks like a military drill instructor. "You were late to practice. I warned you."

"That's not fair," I answer quietly, trying not to show him how angry I am. "It wasn't my fault."

"I said no exceptions, no excuses. Next time, maybe you'll listen."

I can see from his tough expression that there's no possibility of a compromise. I'm doing everything I can not to explode. He's taking away the one thing I have that makes me acceptable to the kids in high school. I can feel blood rushing around my body, heating up. I'm thinking what a *dick* he is. No feelings, no compassion, nothing in his eyes.

"How long do I have to stay out?" I ask.

"I'll let you know. Don't ask me about it again."

This is the worst thing he could have said to me. Not knowing keeps me in a state of high anxiety that I can't come down from.

He turns away, and it's over—for him, anyway. The explosion I've been holding back has now become unavoidable. I tear my helmet off and smash it on the ground. Then I look up into the stands, where my parents are trying to figure out what's going on.

"That's it!" the coach yells back as he walks away. "You're done for the whole game."

I sit on the bench in a daze, watching the other team's offense begin to dominate the game, running right up the center, where I would usually be to stop them. We're getting killed. Every time a play ends, I wait for Coach to signal me into the game, and each time he doesn't, I feel like I'm going crazy. I'm embarrassed and humiliated.

With the building tension and anger, my tics are also going wild, and when halftime comes and I still haven't played, I'm hopping so often that I can hardly keep my balance leaving the field. The coach doesn't seem to notice, or care.

The second half ends, and I haven't been in for a single play. I stumble away from the stadium and, as it turns out, away from football forever.

The new leg tic is the worst I've ever had, and this time it doesn't go away. By the following week, I can't make it on the practice field without falling. *What is happening to me now?*

After that, my school seems to realize the new coach has made a mistake in my case. One of our neighbors with a kid on the team comes over to our house to tell us that the high school is willing to hire a special coach to help me get back on the team.

It doesn't help what my legs are doing now. I'm stumbling and falling a lot. In the end, I would never play high school sports again.

Wheels

Chapter 40

EVEN THOUGH I know it's coming, I'm still surprised when it arrives at our front door. It symbolizes a turning point in my life and is one of my greatest defeats. I hate the thought of it—a *wheelchair!*

Maybe this day would have come anyway, or maybe it's a result of what happened with football. Since I stopped playing, the team has lost almost every game, and my stress seems to have permanently changed the frequency and intensity of my stumbling.

Even so, I think I still get around okay without help, so when the wheelchair is actually brought into the living room and becomes a reality, it makes me feel like someone has taken a giant scoop and hollowed out my insides. I force myself not to cry, but I'm barely holding the tears back.

"Just for a few days, until you don't need it anymore," my mother says to try to calm me down.

"I don't need it *now*, Mom."

"The school thinks you do. They're afraid you might hurt yourself—or somebody else—because you're falling so much."

"That's so unfair. Last week a kid pushed another kid down a flight of stairs, and nobody thought *that* was a big deal."

"They suspended him for doing it."

"Maybe they should make *him* go to school in a wheelchair. That would be fair, right?"

Of course, I end up using the wheelchair. I want to go to school like everyone else, and I won't let anything stop me, even if it means using wheels instead of legs.

Once again I had thought things couldn't get any worse. Guess I was wrong about that.

But in a few days, instead of feeling sorry for myself, I get an idea.

Chapter 41

RIGHT AFTER LUNCH PERIOD, two swinging
doors in a high school corridor burst open faster than
anyone is ready for, and when I come racing through
them in my wheelchair, a bunch of kids scatter to the
sides.

I keep pushing the wheels forward, gathering
speed, and a kid who never paid me any attention
before is suddenly behind me, pushing, too, making
me go even faster.

Just in front of the doors at the far end of the corridor, I step down on the brake lever. The wheels lock

and I come to a skidding stop so hard that I leave rubber skid marks.

By now most of the kids are totally into my fun diversion, the way they are whenever rules are broken. I turn the chair to face them again. I'm the center of the show, the man of the moment, in a different way from the old days. The class clown on wheels.

"Go, Cory," one of the older kids starts chanting. A few more pick up the mantra and urge me on to greater deeds.

"Do it, Cory. Go ahead!" a girl who never seemed to notice me before shouts.

I'm feeling good. I've never gotten this much attention inside the school building. My wheelchair and I have become a source of amusement to the crowd. It's exactly what I wanted.

"C'mon, Cory. One more time."

"Yeah, let's see it."

"Go for it, Cory."

Their cheers require action—and I'm not about to let them down. I jerk back hard on both wheels at the same time. The front of the chair lifts right off the ground. Balancing my weight, I pivot almost completely around in place before touching down again, like a figure skater spinning at the end of his program.

Just about everyone's cheering for me now. No one's ever seen a wheelie like that.

I don't realize it, but as I start to do another one, an adult is racing to the scene. He watches me start to spin. It's someone from the school staff whom I don't know very well. He comes at me so fast that he has to jump to the side to avoid getting cut down by my spinning legs, which stick out from the chair's footrests.

This is way too much for the assembled students, who roar with laughter as a symbol of school discipline is almost knocked down on his rear end. But in a second, the man's angry look sweeps the room and chills the mood.

"Get to your classes," he snaps through his mustache. "Show's over."

All the students head off, and suddenly it's just me and him, and he is breathing hard. "That," he says, "will never happen again."

The next week, my mom drops me off at school the old-fashioned way—on foot. I hop a few times on the way to third period, but I don't fall once. The wheelchair is sitting at home in the garage, just in case. But for now that particular symbol of defeat has been eliminated.

Even though the school was furious with me that

day in the hallway, I think everyone understood that fooling around with the wheelchair was my way of downplaying my physical problems and was not about being reckless or disrespectful.

So why am I walking again and not cruising? I guess the school figured I was more of a danger to myself and the other kids in the wheelchair than I was out of it.

But letting me walk again came with a condition: I wasn't going to be allowed to walk alone. The school was searching for a personal aide to accompany me at all times, wherever I went. But the search was going to be difficult. The job didn't pay well and wasn't much fun.

The other catch was finding somebody who could deal with me.

Me and My Shadow

Chapter 42

IT'S STRANGE GOING to all my classes with a shadow. My shadow's name is Terry. I thought having an aide was going to be humiliating. Now I think of Terry as my best friend in high school.

In addition to helping me get around without hurting anyone, Terry takes notes in my classes. This is especially useful, since I can't write at the speed my teachers talk and my handwriting is like hieroglyphics, anyway. I have poor fine motor skills, or something like that. *Is there anything about me that works right?*

Terry also explains my problems to teachers or

substitutes whenever they forget and think that my tics are a reason for discipline. He's supposed to fix any social problems that may come up, too, like kids making fun of me, but that might be asking too much of anybody.

Terry is kind of a strange guy, and it makes me wonder why all the people who end up in my life are so unusual. He's around forty, with a potbelly and a head that's about two sizes too small for his body. He doesn't like to talk much either. There's something sad about Terry, too. I sometimes wonder how good his life can be when, at his age, he's a nursemaid to a high school kid. I think about what dreams he must have that aren't coming true. I wonder if he ever goes into a rage.

Even so, Terry and I hit it off. He's someone to talk to when I get lonely or upset. He's sympathetic to my problems and stands up for me when somebody gives me a hard time.

But all that starts to change a few weeks into the job. For whatever reason, there's a distance growing between us. He's begun to lose patience with my tics. A few days ago when I started to drum on my desk, he yelled at me to stop. He totally lost it. Terry should have known better. He *did* know better.

Today he's angry with me all the time, and I don't

understand why. And then it gets really out of control. By fifth period, I'm desperate for a cigarette—partly because Terry is getting on my case. I get excused to *secretly* have one. Sometimes Terry comes with me, even though he doesn't smoke, but today he stays behind in the classroom.

I leave by a side door. I'm supposed to walk far away from the building so the other kids can't see me smoke. The school can't officially allow me to have a cigarette on the property, but they mostly look the other way. Twice, teachers who didn't know my situation reported me.

Today I'm a little lazy and figure it doesn't really matter where I smoke, so I go only as far as the gym and take out my pack of Merits. I light one up and suck in a hefty amount of carbon poisons.

Before I can exhale, I hear a voice yelling, "That's it, you're busted."

It's Terry! He jumps out of the shadows of the gym, pointing a finger in my face like it's a gun. He has a triumphant grin, as if he's just uncovered a plot to overthrow the government. It looks like he's having a good time, so I assume he's joking around and take another puff. He keeps shouting that I've broken school rules, and I start laughing, but in a moment I can see I've seriously misjudged the situation.

"You think it's funny? You think this is a big joke? I'm taking you to the principal's office."

I can't believe that Terry means it, but when I don't move, he grabs the cigarette out of my hand and throws it away.

"What are you doing? You know I have to smoke. You're my aide."

"Just shut up," he snaps back, and actually shoves me toward the main office.

I don't understand why this is happening, why Terry of all people would be doing this to me. I feel betrayed and confused.

I thought Terry was my friend. I thought I could trust him.

After the principal listens to Terry's story, he looks up my record, which already includes the other smoking incidents, and he tells me I'm suspended for four days, starting Monday.

"They all know about my smoking," I try to explain. "They understand that I *have* to smoke."

"Who lets you?" the principal wants to know.

I don't want to give him the names of my teachers. "Nobody actually said I could smoke. It's just that they let me."

The principal isn't buying my story. I guess he has

to go by the rules. He's the one who makes up a lot of them.

Terry seems pleased, which I find unbelievable, and so hurtful. Maybe he just can't handle me anymore—my tics are too much for him—and my smoking is a way to be rid of me. Or maybe I'm just a symptom of the life he's sick of.

When we leave the office, I ask him, "What the heck, man? How could you do that to me?"

He just looks at me blankly, his eyes as cold as can be, and keeps walking.

This reaction pushes me too far. Suddenly I'm in a blind fury. I replay the scene over and over and can't stop: him *following* me, *jumping* out of the shadows and reporting me, his *creepy* grin. I want to smash walls. I want to go after him and beat him up, which is funny because I don't know the first thing about fighting and would probably lose. I don't think I've ever felt this much anger toward anyone, and there have been a lot of people who've done cruel things to me.

A plan for some kind of revenge races through my mind, and I do the first stupid thing I can think of. I run to the library computer and e-mail Terry. The angry words just spill out of me—the stronger, the better.

The phone call to my house comes late on Monday, the first day of my suspension for smoking. *The principal wants to see me right away.*

The suspension turns out to be nothing compared to what happens next.

Chapter 43

AT SCHOOL I find out that Terry has read my e-mail and has shown it to the principal. I don't even remember what I wrote, but the message says something about "getting even" and that he'd "better watch out."

"I didn't mean it," I say as soon as I've read it. "I was just mad. He was supposed to protect me at school, not make things worse."

The principal begins speaking differently than he ever has, choosing his words carefully.

"When threats to school personnel are received, they are evaluated by degree. The words you used fall into the third category, a physical threat, and are the most serious. In cases like this, we are required to turn the information over to the county prosecutor for evaluation and possible prosecution."

I sit there, in shock. This must be a bad dream. I've never even heard of a "county prosecutor," but it sounds like I'm being treated as a criminal.

The principal hands my mother a copy of my e-mail. After she reads it, she looks up at me, shaking her head slowly, disappointed but also worried. Now I know I've really crossed the line. I didn't mean to, but it happened.

"You know I'd never do anything like that. I was just letting off steam. I could never hurt anybody."

"I'm afraid that doesn't matter," the principal says. "The legal process has already started. There's nothing I can do to stop it now. The prosecutor has your e-mail."

Chapter 44

TWO DAYS LATER I'm at home, still on suspension for smoking, and going crazy waiting to see what the county prosecutor wants to do. My whole body is ticcing horribly. I don't know what's going to happen to me, and the anxiety is reaching new highs. To settle me down, we try a few different drugs. Neurontin is one of them, used for seizures, but it only makes my tics more crazy. Same thing with Effexor, an antidepressant and mood elevator. It produces wild ticcing, even for me.

"You couldn't have picked a worse time, Cory," my mother says. "There are kids committing violent acts in schools all over America, and you've just threatened your aide. It doesn't matter that you didn't mean it. Everyone's thinking about violence these days."

As usual, I've done the *worst possible thing at the worst possible time.*

"What's going to happen?" I mutter meekly. "Honestly, I would never hurt Terry. You know me, Mom."

She just shakes her head. No pep talk this time.

On the fourth day of my suspension for smoking, my father takes off work to go speak with the director of special education. My poor dad is on the case again. He fills us in when he gets home.

"Mr. Sweeney knows that you're not the kind of person to do something bad, Cory, but what you did was wrong and impulsive. Maybe your aide should have known you weren't really threatening him, but once he complained, you technically could have gotten into real trouble. You're lucky to have the right people on your side."

"And what's going to happen to Terry?" I ask. "I don't want him to be my aide anymore."

"I don't think there's any chance of that happening. But he's still going to be around. The school always needs aides. You know what kind of job it is."

"But it's gonna be okay?" I wish out loud.

"Mr. Sweeney doesn't know yet. He's agreed to ask the county prosecutor to have the serious part of the charges dropped. That's all he could tell me for now."

The next few days are real bad, as my mind fills with dozens of horrible possibilities. Finally the phone rings, and it's Mr. Sweeney from school. I won't be charged with a violent threat. Nothing will go on my record, but I'm being given an additional ten-day suspension. And I have to apologize to Terry. To me, this is the ultimate injustice, but I have no choice.

The first day back at school, I find Terry eating alone in the cafeteria. It isn't easy to even look at him, but I manage to choke the words out.

"Sorry I wrote that e-mail, Terry. It just got me angry 'cause I thought we were friends. I didn't mean what I said. Sorry. I'm really sorry."

When I finish, Terry gets up and leaves without saying a word or even looking at me, as if I'm invisible. Now I feel like a wuss for having groveled, and I have the urge to tell him off again, but I hold myself back—a minor victory.

It's been a few months since the e-mail incident, and Terry and I pass in the halls once in a while. We try not to look at each other. I'm no longer required to have an aide. I'll be more disorganized than I was with Terry, but maybe I'll learn more by having to do things for myself.

By now I guess I should be putting the incident behind me and trying to see Terry's side of the story, but I can't. Even though I acted like an idiot, I still think the wrong person apologized.

The Slippery Slope, Once Again

Chapter 45

IN SOPHOMORE YEAR, it's becoming clear that obsessive-compulsive disorder, or OCD, is a bigger part of my condition than we thought. Right now I'm mostly experiencing the kind of OCD they call *intrusive thoughts*—ideas that can take over your thinking. The worst thought I have now is that there's no point to anything in life. This obsessive idea has suddenly paralyzed my desire to do anything, even to work on my Internet projects.

I feel like I'm drifting outside the world that everyone else is living in, that I'm in a whole different place. I don't understand how other people can feel so attached to their lives and appear to know something I don't. I wonder if they really do or if everybody's just faking it.

"I have a bad thought every day," I tell my parents, "that nothing will ever be any good for me. I look at other people and wonder how they can relax and do normal things, but my thoughts tell me that nothing matters. What am I supposed to do next, and why don't I know? What do I do every day? Am I in hell?"

Over the course of several months, I go from medicine to medicine again, and I also bounce back and forth between three doctors. I don't know if what I'm thinking is caused by the drugs or if another part of my brain is starting to play new games.

My parents learn about Dr. Bonds at a Tourette's syndrome seminar they attend in New York City, where the doctor works. Some people say he would be great for me, so I make the trip to the city twice a week for about five weeks.

Dr. Bonds focuses on my mood as a cause of my other conditions because, he says, a lot of my new thoughts are signs of depression and anxiety. Old and new medicine combinations follow quickly: propranolol and Ativan to relax me, Neurontin (in a different dose than before), Risperdal, and an occasional Xanax when I need it.

It actually seems so normal for me to be popping all these pills every day that I've stopped thinking about it.

The medicines keep changing, but not much about me does. Then, with the reintroduction of Effexor, another antidepressant, I'm suddenly unable to go to school at all. There's a huge increase in my verbal and physical ticcing. I've found another level of hell.

Now the nights are getting as bad as the days because my body isn't letting me rest. One time I'm squirming so much that I have to go to the local hospital for an injection to help me sleep. We're jumping back and forth between Dr. Pressler and Dr. Meyerson, the psychologist who got me out of the psychiatric ward, then back to Dr. Bonds and Dr. Pressler again. From Aricept to Remeron to baclofen. Nothing helps, and now my whole family is depressed. There's no way for me to believe that this isn't my fault, too. Somehow.

At the end of this period of drugs and doctors, I have nothing to show for all the new advice and chemicals that I've been loading into my body. My tics are all over the place, and my OCD is increasing daily. I'm up against a wall and at a new low point in my life.

And I'm running out of medicines to take.

The only thing that's working is alcohol.

Chapter 46

ON A FREEZING SATURDAY NIGHT, I hear someone knock at the basement door. Judging from the pounding, I realize it has to be my friend Mingo, all three hundred pounds of him. Our friendship started in high school when I was on the freshman football team. He was on the varsity and came with some other players to watch me.

Having been on the football team changed a lot of things for me socially. People now think that I'm somebody special. Maybe that's why I have a few regular friends, the *group,* to hang out with. Almost halfway through high school, I still don't go to classes as much as normal kids do, but nothing stops me from having a party with the group. A few of my friends have been calling since school ended on Friday, and some of the talk was about who's supposed to bring the liquor. Of course, I can't be sure anyone is going to show up. Most of the kids I hang out with usually take the best offer at any given moment, and they've ditched me at the last minute more times than I can remember. Sometimes I think that they're my friends mainly because they want what I have...a basement in which to party.

These days Mingo has become the leader of our group. Everyone's afraid of his size, plus he's able to buy liquor for us at a place in another town.

When I open the door, the sight that greets me is pretty ridiculous. Mingo is standing there with another friend of mine, Drew, who's at the opposite end of the size spectrum. Drew is a great guy, but at sixteen, he's very short and weighs fewer than ninety pounds. He could be Mingo's backpack. Of all my so-called friends, I feel the closest to Drew.

Mingo charges in first, carrying a case of beer with a bottle of Jack Daniel's on top of it. He's twenty but looks older, mainly because of his weight, which is increasing all the time now. I worry about his health.

At times Mingo has taken care of me like a brother, teaching me how to do things I should have already learned, like how to dress cool and change the air filter in my car. In return, I buy him things such as a paintball gun or food, and I give him money to purchase liquor. He doesn't get along very well with his family, so a lot of nights my parents let him sleep in my basement. Mingo wasn't exactly an honor student when he graduated from my high school, but he's very street-smart. He'd be the one to bet on in a *Road Warrior* world.

Drew asks if he can play a set on my drums while we're waiting for the others to arrive, and Mingo cracks beers for the three of us. The beers loosen us up, and before long Mingo is hugging me like in the old days. He has a really warm streak, but as close as we are at the moment, Mingo has almost killed me in a few fights over the past year. We get tight for a while, then have a serious argument. That's our pattern, and I have the scars to prove it. Even though my continuing use of Risperdal has piled weight on me, Mingo still outdoes me by a good seventy pounds and has a temper you don't want to set off.

By now I can hear Drew playing some rhythms with feeling on the drums. He is the coolest of us by far, a hippie dude straight out of the sixties. Playing drums unites us. They're a refuge, a way to express our feelings and let out our anger at being different.

Suddenly Sara is standing there. She's come in alone, and I can't help but notice how different she looks from just a year ago. She used to be a thin, pretty blond girl with a sweet smile. Now it hurts me to see that she's become very overweight and reckless. The word is, she's taking whatever she can to get high, even cough syrup. Her values have also changed. At my last party, someone sneaked upstairs from the basement, and I noticed later that a bunch of my Xanax pills were missing from the kitchen cabinet. I can't prove it was she, but it's a solid guess. I should be angry, but I'm not really. I feel sorry for Sara. Drugs can control even a good person's life.

To be honest, my friends have many decent qualities. We have lots of laughs, and when we're just one-on-one, I can count on them. But there are times when they can lie and take things that don't belong to them. They mainly come from poor families or have problems getting along. Since they don't get what they need at home, they live by their wits and hang around people who need them, and I'm one of those people. Also, by now a lot of the nicer kids don't want to be around them, so they are able to attract only one another.

Even though I know all of this, I don't care. I'm with them because it's them or no social life at all. Isolation hurts, and it increases my Tourette's and my OCD, so my parents and I have allowed them to stay in my life, despite the fact that a few of them have ripped me off here and there. Most parents would simply forbid their kids to have such friends. It's been a tough call.

Chapter 47

SARA LIGHTS A CIGARETTE, and I sit down to play my drums and sing to her. A little while later, Robert and Jamie join the party. It's not unusual for us to have four or five guys and only one or two girls at our gatherings.

Jamie is even moodier tonight than the time he stormed out of my house. He's constantly depressed about something that's always right under the surface. Robert is the kid who is most out for himself. He doesn't seem to have much of a conscience, particularly when it comes to sex. To find easy sex, he picks out girls who can't get dates because they're overweight or not too pretty.

Being beautiful, Sara was an exception at first, but when she started going out with Robert, he began to treat her like his other low-self-esteem girls. Now he uses her any time he wants, then gets rid of her. She's so insecure she keeps letting him do what he wants with her.

Sometimes they make out in front of the rest of us, and it kills me to watch this happening. It's like seeing someone spray poison on a beautiful flower. I've always had a close feeling for Sara, and at times I've wanted to be her boyfriend. So it hurts that she has chosen him over me.

I'm surprised to see Eddie come in, because he's never been in our group or to my house before. He's in some of my classes, and I like him, even though we don't really talk. He used to be a good student and a great athlete. But something has happened to Eddie, and I hear that he's become a heavy drinker.

Sara acts glad to see Robert, but he barely says hello to her, and she sinks back into the couch and curls up and looks small. Robert doesn't care. He's in a lousy mood and looks ill. His eyes are sunk deep into his face and he's getting so thin I wonder if he's sick, exposed to something because of all the girls he's screwed.

Mingo opens the Jack Daniel's and asks everyone for money to pay him back, even though it was mostly my money in the first place. Some of the others don't have any money, so I lend it to them. In a little while, everyone feels good. I drink about three big swallows of Jack, then two or three more when the bottle comes around again. I never remember that it takes a while to feel the liquor, so I always drink too much too fast.

This is the biggest party I've had by far. I don't even recognize the two people who come in last. There's a chubby black girl, Angel, who turns out to be one of Robert's new girlfriends. He's invited her without asking me and obviously without caring what it will do to Sara. Angel's friend is a lot prettier. I wonder how they got here. Neither one of them is old enough to drive, so someone must have dropped them off without checking out my party—something my parents would never do.

My basement couch runs wall-to-wall and is filled with people. Eddie takes a seat on the floor, sucking up the bourbon. Sara sits above him and between the couples who are kissing and touching each other all over. It must kill her to see Robert doing this so close to her. At first she acts like she doesn't notice, then she can't take it anymore and grabs the bottle from Eddie and slugs down a huge mouthful.

Even though I'm getting dizzy, I can see how miserable Sara is. When she finally gets up to leave, I put a hand on her shoulder and tell her how shitty Robert is acting and that she doesn't deserve it. I want to hold her and show her there's goodness in the world. She stops and turns to me with a warm, almost inviting look I've never expected to see. I suddenly want to kiss her, and it looks like she wants me to hook up with her. I lean in toward her mouth, but at the last second Angel, the chubby girl I didn't invite, busts in between us looking for the liquor, and the moment has passed. Sara dips away from me and finds the bottle, and the two of them go off laughing.

Chapter 48

AN HOUR LATER, everyone is high. Jamie's mood has taken a turn for the worse, and he slips out without saying good-bye.

Drew is on the drums again while a few of us are outside under the deck in the cold, chilling out. Suddenly there's shouting inside, and I race back in. Apparently Mingo made a move on Angel's friend, who turned him down, and then he tried to hook up with Angel right in front of Robert. Robert is now threatening Mingo, who's cursing him back. So far they are both just yelling, but the whole thing is about to blow, so I step between them.

"Hey, man, that wasn't right!" I shout. "You don't make out with someone else's girlfriend."

Mingo is stunned by my verbal attack, and for a second he just stands there, staring at me. I take his silence to mean that he's seen he was wrong and that the fight is going to end.

"It's just not cool," I press on.

I am so wrong about his mood. I watch as his face gets redder and redder, and in a few seconds I can almost see steam coming off his neck. I try to convince him again, thinking that his loyalty to me and Robert will eventually make him feel bad and quiet him down. Bad call. He's shaking with rage. All I've done is redirect his anger from Robert to me. If I was sober, I might have caught on earlier.

Even in a good mood, Mingo can be a nuclear bomb waiting to go off, and now I've become his detonator. He suddenly lets out a scream and charges me, slamming his elbow into my chest. The impact knocks me off my feet and into the cement wall. He yells that he's going to kill me and looks like he means it, but when the pain hits me, instead of getting scared, I stupidly get angry.

For a split second I move faster than he does and trick him into a headlock. I try to throw him to the floor, forgetting that he's an amazing athlete—and that I don't know how to fight. He easily jerks his head out of my grip and gets me in a bear hug. He squeezes my chest so hard that my breathing is completely cut off, and I can feel my ribs about to snap. Then, all at once, he loosens his grip, curses me, and shoves me full force into a wooden section of the wall that breaks when I hit it.

He stands over me after I fall, breathing hard, waiting to smash me again. His eyes are wild and his forehead is covered with sweat. The person I'm looking at seems insane.

No one else has moved since the fight started. They're all as afraid as I am. Robert is probably glad he's not in my place, although he should have been. In the silence I realize that the drumming has stopped, and suddenly Drew walks in and stands between Mingo and me. He has his hand on Mingo's huge arm, trying to hold him back. Calmly he says, "Chill, bros. Friends shouldn't fight."

Chapter 49

EVEN IN THE MIDDLE of getting beaten up, I can see that this is a really funny scene: Mingo, as big as an elephant, being held back by Drew, who barely comes up to his waist. The ridiculous confrontation is too much for the crowd, and little by little people begin to chuckle. I let out a gasp of relief. Only Mingo still has his fight face on, but in the end he turns away with a grunt.

"You okay, bro?" Drew asks, helping me to my feet.

"Yo, man."

I limp outside to get some air. My ribs feel cracked

and there's blood on my leg, but at least I'm beginning to sober up.

The relief doesn't last for long. Once out the door, I step over a *body* lying on the frozen ground. It turns out to be Eddie, apparently passed out in his own puke. Someone says they haven't seen him move in a long time, and I quickly forget about my ribs.

I bend down to check Eddie's breathing. His face is like ice. He tries to speak, and I can't understand him, but in any case I know he's alive.

The person suddenly standing next to me is my father. He has heard the noise from the fight and has come downstairs in his bathrobe. He is beyond anger and is headed for disgust, but he forces himself to talk softly and deal with the crisis at hand.

"We have to find a way to get him home," he says calmly.

Just then, a car pulls up to the house, and by luck one of the girls in the backseat knows Eddie. My father makes sure the guy who's driving isn't stoned and convinces him to take Eddie home. Together, we lift Eddie to his feet and drag him to the car.

Between this latest drama and the fight, everybody is down and the party is obviously about to end. I'm feeling really depressed, and I'm hurting inside as much as I'm hurting outside.

After everyone leaves, my father and I stand in the basement room, checking out the wreckage of the evening—the bottles, the spilled ashtrays, the broken wall, all of it. He stares into my bloodshot eyes with a look I've seen many times before and just shakes his head. He's too depressed to speak.

"Sorry, Dad" is all I can manage to say.

He is someplace else in his mind when he answers, "It's okay, I know you didn't want this either. Go to bed. We'll clean up in the morning."

I know what he's really thinking: *Never again. This is the last time. The last party.*

Of course, it won't be. Even at this moment, we both know that in my life it's either times like this or nothing at all. And "nothing at all" is worse.

Two hours later, I'm asleep when the phone rings, and my mother says it's for me. It's a social worker at the emergency ward of the local hospital. Sara has been admitted there with an overdose of something and is having her stomach pumped. She's given them my number, not her own family's.

I tell my parents what's happened and that I have to help her, and then I'm off to spend a few hours at the hospital, at the bedside of my good friend Sara.

Another Saturday night with friends.

Chapter 50

THE CONTRASTS ARE GETTING really crazy; they'd be too extreme for anybody to handle, let alone a teenager. Last night I passed out from drinking in my basement. Tonight I'm doing seventy miles per hour on my street-legal dirt bike and I'm lost somewhere on the New Jersey Turnpike.

It's ten o'clock on an August night. I'm in a pouring rain and can barely see where I'm going.

School is out for the summer, and all I want to do is ride. Even though I'm pretty out of it from all the medicine I'm on, the thrill of riding brings me back to life with a rush of adrenaline. This is all about life . . . or maybe the opposite. Dirt bikes and motorcycles have been an obsession of mine ever since I can remember. When I ride, I move in a way I can't anywhere else. It feeds my need for danger. I can see myself in the future, riding all the time, never having to worry about school or jobs or friends, never having to explain myself to anyone.

A sudden compulsion to test *just how close I can get to crashing* makes me jerk the handlebars to the right, almost to the point where I lose control. I should be scared out of my mind, but the thrill makes me do it again, this time a little farther to the right, just to see how much I can get away with.

The bike shudders and starts to slip out from under me. The wheel is angled near the point of no return, but I just manage to get control back.

Tonight I started out on a peaceful ride on dry local streets, but I've gotten lost and now I'm trapped in a nightmare on the turnpike.

I have the option of pulling off the road, but that will leave me in the middle of nowhere and I'll never get home. Also, it would be dangerous. I'm in the fast lane, and the traffic on my right is a high-speed stream of cars and trucks. I drop the speed down to around forty in an attempt to cut over, but the drivers behind me lean on their horns, so I give the bike more throttle again.

The stinging rain starts to get heavier, and I can't see anything. This is crazy dangerous.

My helmet doesn't have a visor and I'm wearing only a light sweater because I didn't plan to be here, or in the rain. There's no chance of being rescued by my parents because I don't have a cell phone. My hands are so cold I can hardly feel them, and I wonder whether my fingers will work at all the next time I use the hand brake.

At this point I've been lost on different highways for two hours, and there's almost no gas left in my tank. Every new road has taken me farther away from home until I've ended up here, *wherever I am*. I'm sure that somehow I'll get out of this. I always do. But I'm also scared about the odds of it ending in a horrible accident. Every biker has at least one, they tell me. And often *only one*.

When the turn-the-wheel compulsion comes again, I do a substitution tic, an idea given to me by one of the therapists I've had.

Instead of twisting the handlebars, I arch my back until I'm lifted completely out of the seat. This makes me steer with my fingertips, but at least I'm not skidding.

People passing me must think I'm the dumbest driver ever, doing stunts in these conditions, risking my life for no reason. I wish it was only a stunt.

In the distance I see a toll plaza coming up fast, and I squeeze the hand brake tightly instead of using my foot brake. I'm not thinking clearly. How could I be? My bike pulls sharply to one side, and for a few frightening seconds I'm totally out of control. Though my dirt bike has been adapted for the street, it's made for off-road riding and is too light for the highway and for this speed. But the thrill of velocity always wins out over sanity. At the last moment, the thick tire tread catches hold of the pavement and the bike is stable again.

By now I've had enough and need help bad. I'm in way over my head. My body is numb from the cold, and I have no hope of finding my way home by myself.

When I pull up to the tollbooth, I ask the man inside for help, but he doesn't seem to hear me and only asks for money. I haven't got any because I've spent it all on the other tolls.

While he's writing down my name and address, a miracle happens. A woman in the lane next to me rolls down her window and asks if I need help. It must have been obvious to her that I was in bad shape.

Someone is watching over me on this night, because it turns out that the woman lives in my hometown. This is the best news I've heard in my entire life. She tells me to follow her home.

Forty minutes later when I walk into my house, my parents are crazy with worry. I look like I've been swimming and have turned blue from the cold. When I tell my story, they shake their heads in disbelief. This is just another in a series of disasters I've been involved in over the years. Some of them have given my mom migraines. I hope this one won't.

Before I take a hot shower, I need a drink, a real one. After what I've been through, my father hasn't got the heart to say no and pours one for each of us.

In a little while the steam from the hot shower transports me to another place. My mind has seized on a Beach Boys song about traveling around the world, and it plays over and over again. *Bermuda, Bahama, come on, pretty mama.*

I close my eyes and see myself back on the highway.

The road is smooth and dry and endless. The sun is out, and I'm going faster than I ever have. There is no sense of danger, just pure joy.

My bike and I are flying.

Flying in the wind.

End of the Line

Chapter 51

IT'S NEAR THE MIDDLE of my junior year, and everything is pretty bad again. I'm acting reckless and don't care what I say to people, which is only pushing them farther away. There are too many nights spent drinking on the basement couch until I pass out. My parents are trying to stop me, but they can't, because I lie and won't listen to them. And because they don't know any other way for me to get some peace either.

I'm hopelessly behind in my schoolwork. I'm fat and a chain-smoker. I'm depressed over not being able to change my life.

My worsening condition is having a big effect on

Jessie, too. She's always said she wants to teach special-needs kids, and I think that growing up with me is probably one of the main reasons. Now she's decided to teach people with Down syndrome. I know she's serious because last summer she coached a Special Olympics team with severely handicapped kids and grown-ups. Some of them were in wheelchairs and some had been born without parts of their bodies. She loved helping them and they loved her and chanted *Jessie, Jessie,* every morning when they saw her arriving. She has a real gift as a teacher and coach. This seems to be the only good thing that's come out of what's been happening to me.

In the past four months I've had two new doctors, which brings the total to more than a dozen. The latest one believes that OCD is the main cause of my body movements. He says that most people with Tourette's also have some OCD, but like everything else about me, my OCD isn't the typical kind.

I don't have to wash my hands over and over, or go in and out of doorways dozens of times. And I'm not a checker who has to keep going back to make sure they've done things such as turn off the stove or lock the doors.

But all OCD people get *stuck* on their compulsion. The new doctor's theory is that Tourette's starts my body doing something, and then instead of being able to let the tic shut off, I get caught on the movement because of the OCD. My OCD gets stuck on my Tourette's.

Looking back now, I wonder if a lot of the things I did were more symptoms of OCD than Tourette's—like my need in elementary school to form my letters perfectly and put them in exactly the right place on the lines.

My doctor believes that my high level of anxiety is also intensifying everything else. Still, with all his good thinking, so far his medicines aren't working any better than anyone else's.

One smart thing he does is to help me get off Risperdal for good. I'd been living in a thick fog and had been unaware of it. It was as if a sudden wind blew it all away. I'd had no idea how drugged out I was from the Risperdal. Now at least I feel connected to the world. Unfortunately, I'm also more in touch with the reality of what my life has become.

In an attempt to stabilize my mood, I start taking Zyprexa, another antipsychotic used to treat bipolar disorder and mania. At first my body calms down a lot, but the drug makes me very angry. Paxil is back again, too, but it stops working after two weeks and makes me even angrier. My whole life is like a movie about kids on drugs, but my drugs are supposed to be good for me.

My doctor's thinking prompts a flow of new drugs into my mouth. The bottles litter our house, with most of the pills still untaken: Geodon, Lamictal, Seroquel, Topamax. I'm so desperate I even go back to tetrabenazine, this time in a much smaller dose, until it again makes life too miserable for most people to even imagine.

Nothing works.

Nothing works.

Nothing ever works.

This isn't me just repeating and getting stuck on the same words. This is reality.

Finally, based on the radical theory that we should try to do the opposite of everything we'd done before, the doctor wants to prescribe pergolide, a drug that would increase the chemical in my brain that we've always thought was one of the problems. This seems to be a desperate move a doctor makes only when he thinks you're at the end of the road. *Is that where I am?*

Maybe pergolide is the radical solution we've been looking for, but by now I've had it. I decide not to find out. I'm finished, wiped out, sick of being a walking medicine cabinet, tired of symptoms and side effects. I like being clear and awake, and I never want to be in the fog again. This is where I draw the line, and my family finally agrees with me.

It's over. No more drugs.

Except, of course, the only one that's ever worked: *alcohol*.

Chapter 52

I TAKE ANOTHER MOUTHFUL OF VODKA and feel a warm wave spreading through my body. The serenity that liquor brings is better than any medicine I've ever taken and is the only way I get relief from my restless body. I'm not worried about the consequences of liquor anymore. I know they can't be any worse than the consequences I experience every day without it.

Lying on the basement couch, I think about where I've ended up. My junior year of high school continues to be more of a disaster than the end of my sophomore year. I'm not going to school much because I'm unable to sit still or concentrate on what my teachers are saying. My obsessive need for nicotine makes it worse. Noises are constantly coming out of my mouth that no one can deal with. My friends call only when they want something, and my compulsions are making me hurt myself again. I have scars and bruises everywhere.

Tonight I need to feel better any way I can, and I'm finally drifting off into a deep, drunken sleep.

Somewhere around three or four in the morning, I'm aware of having a hard time breathing. I start coughing but not enough to wake up completely. When the coughing becomes almost continuous, I can feel my lungs burning, which eventually forces me out of my stupor.

My eyes open to a room thick with a new and unusual haze. When I look for the source, I see smoke coming from the couch cushion beneath me. Maybe the entire couch. There's a glowing red circle two feet in diameter that slowly spreads as I watch. The edge of the fire is only an inch from my arm. In the middle of the circle are the charred remains of a cigarette filter that had dropped away from my mouth when I fell asleep.

I'm setting the whole house on fire!

Chapter 53

I LEAP OFF THE BURNING COUCH, afraid that at any second the whole thing will burst into flames and set fire to the walls of our house. My mind fills with horrifying images. The fire will become an inferno that will break through the ceiling and blaze up the first-floor stairs. My sister will be asleep in her room when the smoke and flames pour in too fast, and she will be unable to get up and run. The fire will then rip across the hall to my parents' room.

The instinct to scream catches in my throat. I don't want my family to find out what I've done. There has to be a way to stop this disaster myself.

I don't know what to do, though. I should still be drunk, but I'm stone-cold sober and totally aware of what's happening.

In a moment the first wave of terror subsides, and I run across the room to where the smoke is thinner. I take a deep breath and look back at the couch. The fire hasn't spread yet, but any breeze will make it burst into a blaze I'd never be able to put out. *Seconds, only seconds.*

I race back and rip the cushions from the couch. The fire has burrowed deep inside, to the couch's inner padding. There's no chance of putting it out by beating the cushions.

I'm coughing so hard that I can barely breathe. I'm also scared out of my mind.

I look around the room for another answer and spot the bottle of vodka that I'd half emptied before falling asleep. I grab it and pour what's left onto the cushions. The fire hisses loudly but doesn't go out. Then I realize how crazy that was. *Alcohol on a fire?* The vodka could have ignited. I was stupid and lucky.

But the liquor *is* making things worse. It's creating a terrifying amount of dense black smoke. My eyes are burning and watering so much I can hardly see. I'm coughing and gagging.

Get the fire out of the house.

Holding the burning cushions in front of me, I make a run for the back door. The thickest part of the smoke streams back directly into my face. I'm forced to inhale it before it has time to mix with the air outside. I'm suffocating now, and I can't see where I'm going. The room is dense with smoke and the windows are all shut.

I feel my way to the far wall and fumble for the exit. My hand finds the dead bolt, but the old door is warped. The lock won't turn unless the door is forced back into its frame.

Finally the door bursts open, and I charge outside and hurl the smoking cushions as far as I can into the backyard.

For the first time since I woke up, clean, fresh air pours into my lungs, but somehow that makes me cough even more.

When I can breathe again, I go back into the room to check for more fire. The smoke makes the search impossible, so I open the windows on two sides of the room. Cold air rushes in one side and sucks smoke out the other. At first I don't know why the smoke detectors aren't going off, but then I remember there aren't any in the basement.

In a few minutes the room is nearly clear of smoke,

and my knees feel too wobbly to hold me up. I make it back to the couch frame and collapse. My clothes, my skin, and the whole room reek of smoke. The basement has become freezing cold, but the worst is over. I hope, anyway.

There's still no sound from upstairs. No one has awakened. They don't have a clue how close they came to disaster, how close I came to killing everybody.

Alone in the eerily silent room, I close my eyes, not to sleep but to play back the movie that is my life, to see what is still worth saving inside of me. Amazingly somewhere I can sense hopefulness. It's like the start of a gentle rain in a desert that's been dry for years — *since I was almost five, for God's sake!*

There's anger, too, but not the kind that leads to my rage attacks. *This is an anger that can be used and channeled.*

The idea of fighting back comes with such urgency that I want to write it all down — so I can think about it when I wake up again.

I find a pencil and paper in the workroom and don't finish until my muscles are cramped from sitting in the same position. As it starts to get light outside, I finally fall asleep on the remnants of the same couch that almost took away my family's world and maybe my life.

My mother finds me in the morning, still asleep in the frozen room. The windows are wide open, the stinging smell of the burning couch still thick in the air. I'm on my back, stretched out full length. My arms are folded over my chest. Under them is a smudged yellow legal pad on which I have scrawled this letter to myself:

I was born with the worst disease.

My body wants me to suffer.

My whole life, I've been gasping for air.

The ground hasn't ever been there.

I've been trying to fly when I can't even breathe.

There's been nothing to build on, not even a dream.

You probably can't comprehend it. And I don't blame you.

You're only human and have only smelled the slightest micro-atom of what I breathe. My life has been the most disgusting and vile thing you could imagine. My body wants to hurt me. I can't stop breaking myself down, physically and mentally.

I have severely damaged my teeth. Ticced so hard I've broken my ribs. My wrists scream with pain. My neck burns and aches.

I'm so tired, yet I still have to fight. I could explode. I want to go to war and kill bad shit.

Yet I am reminded that my life has been only that of prison and torturous pain.

My own body has betrayed me. I can't feel safe with myself.

Right now I want to smash my head through the computer screen and explode myself with the sharp huge bang of a shrapnel bomb. Liquefy me and burn me to ash. Then dump water on my ashes and get RID of them.

My anxiety is so high I can't even make sense of anything.

I've lost the world. I've lost the world.

I'm in myself and can't get out.

The world's joy makes me feel like an outcast.

I'm worn ragged, dirty, no good, hopeless, disgusting, insane.

But I am alive. I am alive.

I still have human feelings and needs.

I have dreams.

Don't desert me any longer, common goodness. How can you? You've already committed the biggest sin imaginable. Taking a good-hearted, peaceful, intelligent person and making him come within a millimeter of taking his own life.

Am I insane? It would seem so. I can't stop hurting myself.

My parents don't know what I've gone through. If they did, they'd be saying every word to me as if it were their last.

I deserve the world.

And I am stronger than the worst things that happen to me.

I am not suicidal.

I will take control of my OCD.

I will fight and KILL my Tourette's.

Rip them apart or be doomed.

I will own my own mind.

I will never give up.

Fuck you, OCD.

The war has NOW BEGUN.

And you're already bleeding.

I will survive.

I will love life, if life will love me.

Part Four

THE INTERVENTION

Chapter 54

DAY 1

The temperature is fifteen below zero. Trust me on that—it could be lower by now. There's nothing between me and the snow except my sleeping bag and a four-foot-square tarp mounted on sticks over my head.

I'm a mile up in the mountains of Wyoming, a few hundred miles northeast of the 2002 Olympic Winter Games, which have just started in Salt Lake City.

It's my first morning at Roundtop Wilderness Camp for troubled teens.

The noise of an unseen, unidentified animal nearby

in the woods wakes me from an uncomfortable sleep. When I try to open my eyes, I find they're welded shut by a crust of ice. I pry the frozen stuff away, one small particle at a time. A few pieces come off with my eyelashes embedded in them.

I'm not here because of my doctors. None of them has ever advised that I do something this unusual, or this extreme.

After discovering the dangerous fire in the basement, my parents knew they had to intervene. They eventually came up with the idea of wilderness camp after hearing about a good experience some friends of theirs had had with their son. Shocked by my own actions that night, and realizing what could happen if I went on that way, I was ready to try anything.

Even this.

They call places like these *camps,* as though they're an outdoor adventure, like Outward Bound. Before I arrived, I actually thought this would be fun, but last night at my first campfire meeting, I found out the truth. This will *not* be fun. Maybe to *read* about but not to live through.

"Wilderness is for guys like you who have a lot of trouble making it on the outside," the head counselor announced at the meeting.

He was around thirty, the oldest of the staff of four

with our group. The others looked young enough to be in college, although I doubted they were.

"Most of you have been in trouble with the police, your families, or your schools. You've done violent things, used or sold drugs, stolen stuff or set fires.

"We're here to help you fix your lives, but in the end it's going to be you who have to do it."

I looked around at the six other kids at the camp, most of whom were my age or younger. A few of them arrived here *escorted,* which is a nice way of saying that they were brought by law-enforcement officers because they wouldn't come any other way. One of them arrived in handcuffs.

I'm different from the others, except for my addiction to alcohol and cigarettes. I'm not a bad kid. The closest I came to being in trouble was when I wrote that e-mail to Terry. And maybe almost burning down our house.

"The rules are simple," the counselor went on. "You'll be on this mountain for as long as it takes to work out your problems. No more, and no less. The time you're here depends on your progress and your ability to work as part of a group. Some of you will be here for one cycle, others longer. That's the deal, guys."

I was stuck on one part of his speech: *for as long as*

it takes to work out your problems. The threat that there was no telling how long I would have to be here was very frightening. Ricky, the kid sitting on the left, told me that he'd been on the mountain for three months and was doing this cycle over again.

Does that mean I could be here for months? Or a year? What's to stop me from being here forever? I had to fight off a sudden wave of panic. And tics, of course.

"The conditions here are very basic," the counselor continued. "We've brought enough food with us to get by, and we'll use what we find in this terrain for shelter to survive the cold. We'll teach you how to do this. This is a year-round program, but winter is the hardest. Your bad luck. If we work as a group, we make it. If we don't, we all suffer. Everybody got that?"

No one responded. This wasn't like a classroom back in school. These guys were a tough, hardened bunch. Maybe encounters with the police made them that way.

The silence made me really nervous and uncomfortable. I felt as if I had to say something to break the tension. But it was obvious that this would be a mistake.

"Don't even think of trying to get away from here,"

the head guy went on. "The closest human beings are twenty miles away on a military post. They know about this program and are on the alert for anyone who shows up in their area. That doesn't really matter because even if you got away, you'd probably never make it there in this weather. But even if you did, you wouldn't like what happened to you next."

This last speech erased any doubt that any of us were going to escape from this place on our own.

Another, longer silence fell over the group. Reality was setting in for everybody. *Wilderness camp.* We got it now.

"Are there any questions so far?" the counselor asked when he was done spelling out the rules.

After a long wait with no one saying anything, my urge to do something inappropriate rose to the point where it was unstoppable, and at once I found myself shouting, "Run! Run!"

My unbelievably disrespectful and rebellious command shattered the stillness of the deadly serious moment. I couldn't believe I'd said it any more than the rest of the group could. At first, everyone stared at me, openmouthed. I didn't know how to explain what made me do it. I wondered if the word *compulsion* meant anything to them.

"I'm sorry . . . I didn't mean . . ." was all I could get out before the two junior counselors were on either side of me.

"Take off your boots, wise guy," the bigger of the two said to me. "You're not going anywhere."

Chapter 55

DAY 3

My sleeping bag is covered by a good half foot of snow, which has been falling steadily throughout the night. It's wet on the inside from ice that I must have brought in on my coat before passing out from exhaustion.

In my hurry to get out of the cold, I also left the bottom of the bag open to the wind, and now I can't feel my right foot. I wonder if it's been asleep too long to ever come back to normal.

If I had my boots on, I'd stand and jump up and down to try to get some feeling back in my foot, but they take away our boots at night in case anyone is still thinking about escaping—like they took mine that first night. I'm cold to the bone and hungry. If I'd known what it was going to be like here, I would have probably needed one of those escorts to get me to the camp.

What they said the first night has turned out to be absolutely true. The idea of this place is very simple: force troubled kids to cooperate in order to survive, and get us through the withdrawal period of our addictions by having us focus instead on more immediate issues—like eating, going to the bathroom in the woods, and not freezing to death.

I'm not the first person who's come here with an alcohol addiction, but I'm the first with that plus Tourette's and OCD.

Before I came up on the mountain, the people who run the place said they didn't know if I could make it, but they were willing to give it a try. My main worry is that sometimes my tics are so bad I can hurt myself and then I can't move without excruciating pain. If that happens, I won't be able to keep up and they'll send me home. The more I'm up here, the more tempted I am to fake my tics for just that reason, but I've promised myself I won't do that.

If I go back home the way that I came, there's nothing in my old life to help me.

So every time one of my tics makes me think of giving up, I tell myself that I'm not going to let it beat me. I can't. This is life-and-death for me, and not just because of the temperature and the amazing amount of snow.

Chapter 56

DAY 5

A terrible thought has begun to take over my mind. It's been in the back of my head since the second day, but now it's risen to the surface and I can't think of anything else. *My father has been killed in a plane crash on his way home from the wilderness camp. Or he and my mother both died after he got home.*

There is no other explanation for why my parents haven't contacted me. In my whole life, I've never been away from them for this long. They've never even had a vacation away from me. The idea that they wouldn't even try to see how I'm doing in this dangerous place is impossible—*unless something bad has happened to them.*

The counselors haven't brought it up either, and I think it's because they must know something and are hiding it. I'm so preoccupied with this fear that it's begun to slow me down from doing the normal chores required as part of group survival.

Finally the thought makes me so frantic that in the middle of a task I break the rule about leaving my area and force a conversation with Kevin, the head counselor.

"I'm scared that something has happened to my parents," I say without wasting time. "I'm not kidding, I'm serious."

"It's possible," he answers casually. "I don't know."

His calmness shocks me. "I have to find out. I need to know. I have a bad feeling."

He shakes his head. "You're here and you have to make it work on your own, no matter what. I think I explained all that the first night."

I can't believe he's not trying to talk me out of my fear, to reason with me like all my other doctors have. He's not nasty or mean, just firm and very clear.

On one level I understand why he is acting this way, and that it doesn't mean he knows something. But on the way back to my work area, I'm still terrified about my parents, and now there's nothing I can do about it. Obviously, he's right. I am on my own in every way up here, and the fact that I don't know for how long makes things a hundred times worse for someone like me. It's a perfect formula for the panic that bubbles near the surface all the time.

I'm cold, exhausted, and always hungry, and I miss home so much I sometimes want to cry, but I won't let myself. Kevin has forced me to recognize I have only two choices: throw myself on the ground and give up and let them send me home, or fight off the bad thoughts as best I can and do what I have to do to survive.

Trying to analyze my situation a little, I realize that I haven't needed a drink or a cigarette almost the whole time I've been here. As hard as this experience has been, maybe I'm really starting to do something for myself. With everything I've always needed suddenly taken away from me, hey, I'm still alive.

And that's when, for the first time, I start thinking about something really impossible.

As bad as it is, this is good.

Chapter 57

DAY 7

As dawn breaks, the others around me are already out of their sleeping bags.

We've all spent the night close enough to be in touch in case of a storm but far enough apart so there's no verbal contact. The guys are all busy trying to light a fire but not with matches. For whatever reason, we have to do it the way the Indians did, rubbing a stick between our hands into a groove in a piece of wood until it smolders into an ember, then quickly putting some dried grass on it and blowing to get a flame.

We need the fire for more than warmth. It melts our drinking water, which freezes every night, and is also used for all our cooking. If we can't make a fire, we can't eat the cornmeal, soy, and millet they've given us in small bags.

Today it takes me so long to get my boots on that there isn't time to try to make my own fire. When I get enough ice off my boots to get into them, I realize that one of my gloves is missing, and I spend another precious few minutes looking for it. Finally, one of the counselors gives me another glove but says it will be the last. This is the third time I've lost a glove — in two days.

I walk out into the woods to go to the bathroom, then come back and start to clean up my area.

By the time I get to the common kettle, the rest of the guys are already finished eating and about to put out the fire. Nobody makes fun of me, but nobody offers to help either. That's okay.

I get some water, but there's no breakfast for me this morning because I haven't contributed to the effort. Back at my sleeping bag, I stuff some raw corn-meal into my mouth, then spit it out when it makes me gag.

The lead counselor gathers us together and checks each person's gear. By now everyone else is carrying their possessions in a backpack they've made themselves, shaping it with branches and holding it together with strips of rawhide. The backpack is crucial to survival because there's no other way to carry the supplies that keep us going.

It takes most people a day or two to make a backpack. I've been working on mine since I got here, and it's still not holding together enough to carry much. Until I make it better, I'm hand-carrying some of my stuff, which partly explains why I keep losing certain items over and over, like my gloves.

As the sun comes up from behind a nearby mountain, everyone assembles with their gear. One of the counselors tells us about the day's activity plan.

"We're going on a little hike today, nothing too hard," he announces. "Just a few miles, straight up the mountain."

He conveniently forgets to add, *in knee-deep snow.*

Chapter 58

DAY 12

Since that first time we climbed up the mountain, we've made a big trip every single day. Now we're going to stay in base camp for a while, so we're digging ditches that will serve as latrines and will ensure that we don't contaminate the area around us.

The only tools we have are the jagged stones we've been able to pry out of the frozen ground. Using them to dig is backbreaking work, and it takes several hours to show very little in the way of results.

We are also completing a clearing in the woods for a future campsite for another group. We've found a patch of land rising above the snow that doesn't have much growing on it, and we have to figure out how to cut down what's left.

One of the tics I've feared the most has suddenly returned — the need to twist my ribs back until something hurts inside of me. I've been doing it all day and have either torn something in my chest again or pulled a muscle.

I'm having trouble breathing, but I don't want to use that as an excuse to stop working. I'm part of the group now, and they've accepted me, so I want to do my share.

I've also had to make my rope belt tighter again; my pants have dropped to my ankles a few times because I've lost so much weight. I still miss at least one meal a day because I'm usually too frozen or tired to prepare it, and I'm burning calories from working and trying to stay warm in the freezing climate. I'm even burning calories because of my tics.

Despite the extreme cold, the bottoms of my layered shirts get soaking wet from sweat. It's no wonder I can feel myself getting thinner. I imagine what I would look like in a mirror. But of course there are no mirrors.

For some reason the skin on the back of my hands is turning black. I don't know if I'm just dirty or if that is an early sign of frostbite. I've lost so many gloves that they've stopped giving them to me sometimes. They think that this will make me learn to keep track of them better, but I'm just too disorganized. Or maybe too forgetful. It usually takes a lot of mistakes, and suffering a lot of consequences, before I learn any lesson.

Chapter 59

DAY 16

We're halfway up the mountain. Today, we've been walking for six hours with only short rests for water and a break for lunch that took longer than planned. I finally get to eat some cooked soy and cornmeal, which tastes like the best steak I've ever had. I still haven't finished making my backpack strong enough, and carrying some of my supplies in my arms has been almost impossible, especially in the rougher terrain.

Part of the trip is over bare rocks swept clean by a strong wind, and part is in waist-deep snow. My famous hopping tic is severe today, and when I hop in the deep snow, I often fall and there's no one to pick me up. But at least the snow softens the blow.

"We're way behind schedule," one of the counselors tells us halfway through the day. "If we get any slower, we won't reach our camp and you won't like where you have to sleep tonight. You won't like it at all!"

This is not the greatest threat in the world. We already don't like where we sleep.

But lying out in the open is dangerous at this higher altitude, where it's much colder. Before dark we have to get to a level place much higher up that will serve as our campsite for the night and that will be safe from the big snowstorm that's supposed to be coming.

Another serious problem arises around four o'clock. The water we're carrying has frozen solid, and because we're so far behind, there's no time to stop and thaw it out. A few mouthfuls of snow every now and then keep us from getting dehydrated.

When we get to the campsite it's almost dark, and by the time I've laid out my sleeping bag and set up my tarp, my hands are too frozen to work on a fire. As hungry as I am, I'm too tired to eat. I take my boots off and crawl into my sleeping bag, missing a second meal in one day.

I have to sleep within view of two counselors who are watching from about fifty yards away. I pray they don't ask me to get out of my sleeping bag, and they don't. But in the morning they tell me that if I don't get my act together and finish the hike, I'll be in the wilderness for a long time.

Or be kicked out.

With all that I'm going through, I'm once again astonished to find myself thinking that this is the worst that can happen.

Chapter 60

DAY 20

Miraculously, I'm at the top of the mountain as the sun is setting. I'm the last to arrive, but I got here.

The backpack, which took me more than two weeks to assemble, isn't anything to brag about, but it actually holds together pretty well, and all my supplies have made it with me. Tonight I will sleep in this frigid air with a smile on my face and food in my stomach.

The beauty of the place is amazing, especially the light and the quiet peacefulness. I feel like I'm at the top of that tree again, the one I climbed back at my house years ago. Maybe that's the way I have to find the answer—I need to be on my own like this, and to push hard in order to relax and be myself. Now I can spend hours looking at the patterns of the night-time shadows in the snow, the way the white-coated treetops are lit up by the sun and the moon.

As tired as I am, being here is exhilarating.

I am living life on a very basic level. Its calming effect is stronger than any medicine I've ever taken.

I haven't wanted a drink...or my medicines... since the very first night. The air is so pure here that the idea of putting cigarette smoke into my lungs seems outrageously dumb and disgusting.

The worst of my wrenching body movements have also lessened, either because I've been so distracted or because the exertion has tired me out. I deal only with the rituals of survival and the simple jobs that make it possible. *I'm making it.* I think of nothing else.

In some ways, my past life seems like it was a hundred years ago and happened to a different person. When I do think of my friends, I feel sorry for the smallness of their average days and wish they could experience what I have. I've been able to put aside threatening intrusive thoughts, like the idea that something has happened to my parents. I'm going on faith that it is just my mind trying to trap me in a bad loop again.

As I've grown stronger, I've become thinner and thinner. My clothes are practically falling off me and the rope is tight around my waist to keep my pants on.

My depression is lifting, too. I'm learning that I'm able to endure terrible hardship. This is an amazing feeling of power that I know will help me fight whatever comes at me after I leave. I've always believed I had inner strength, but I never thought it would be tested in such a profound and crucial way.

There is no doubt that this has been the worst thing I've ever had to do, the worst place my parents could possibly have sent me to.

And the best thing that has ever happened to me.

Chapter 61

DAY 23

The pickup truck arrives at base camp just after noon.

I will be its only passenger.

I shake hands with each of the other kids and the counselors who have assembled to say good-bye, my brothers in the wilderness. There is a mutual respect and an unspoken jealousy felt by the other campers. Some of them will stay for a few more weeks. The one who has already been here for four months still has no idea when he's leaving.

But I'm going home.

Before getting into the truck, I turn for a last look up at the snow-covered mountain that I climbed when my body kept trying to stop me. I've suffered more here physically than I ever thought possible.

I'm leaving the mountain a different person than I was when I arrived. I've lost sixty pounds and am free of my addictions. I am stronger inside and out and have gotten past fears that none of the medicines I've taken could conquer.

My tics haven't left, but now they are more like nuisances, not overwhelming problems.

Mainly, I feel as if I can do anything I set my mind to.

The trip down the mountain takes a half hour on trails barely wide enough for our vehicle. Eventually the snowpack gets thin, and there are patches of dirt and bleached-out grass here and there.

Soon after that, we get to a rough country dirt road that leads back to the main street and the modest two-story house that serves as the camp's headquarters.

There are a bunch of new teenagers on the front lawn, boys and girls about my age fixing up sleeping bags for their trip to the mountain. They look fresh and rosy cheeked and seem like nice kids, but I know they're here because they've got problems. I wonder if they understand what lies ahead. I wonder if they'll be able to make it.

As I pass them, they stare at the kid with blackened hands who is back from weeks of cold and deprivation but is walking tall.

I turn from them to go into the house, and I see my father standing outside, waiting for me. He sees me and waves. "Hey," he calls. In the end, no matter what, he's always there. My mind is flooded with a thousand thoughts, but mostly I am proud. A big grin spreads over my face as I reach out for him.

He holds me and grabs my shoulder tightly. "You did it."

When we hug, I can feel his body shaking with emotion, almost as much as mine.

Chapter 62

I SIT ACROSS THE TABLE from an absolutely beautiful teenage girl who breaks my heart every time I look at her. I'm at the adolescent OCD ward of the world-famous Wellington Neurological Center, a thousand miles from where my father picked me up at the bottom of the mountain.

Six of us patients are in the cafeteria to eat lunch, but what Noelle is doing is like nothing I've ever seen in my life. It kills me just to watch.

Noelle is a teenager from somewhere in Canada. She has long black silken hair and flashing eyes with dark circles under them that must be there because she doesn't sleep much. Her parents have sent her all over the world for different kinds of treatments, and none of them has helped. She's been at the clinic for a long time, and from what I can see, she shows no signs of getting out.

I try not to stare as she picks up a small portion of food from her plate, then stops the movement of her fork after lifting it only a few inches. She holds the fork there for as long as it takes her to complete some unknown counting ritual or some need for symmetry.

After about twenty seconds, she gathers herself for another move. A second lurch of her right arm brings the fork higher, but she stops it before it gets to her mouth. Something else must be completed in her mind before she can go any farther.

Finally, when she is able to get the food into her mouth, she chews and swallows in a certain regulated way. It's exhausting just to watch her. And so damn sad that I can barely stand it.

Noelle has multiple obsessive-compulsive rituals so complex that it can take her more than a minute to eat a single bite of food. Getting through a simple meal takes forever, and she usually doesn't finish because time runs out.

By now the rest of us have gotten used to eating

with her, but today's lunch is so protracted that we'll miss our therapy sessions if we don't leave. So finally the aide who has come with us gently urges her to stop.

Noelle does what she's told with a gracious smile, and slowly she lowers the fork to her plate. My heart breaks for her again. She must be incredibly embarrassed by what she has to do, but she doesn't show it. I'll never get used to watching her go through so much hell just to feed herself.

Despite her sickness, Noelle is amazingly smart, maybe genius level. I've been told that she can speak four languages, but she's so deeply afflicted with her ritual disorders that her intelligence isn't any help to her right now. These days she usually just sits there, her eyes wide open in a dazed, sometimes frightened look, and seems almost paralyzed. She might say a few words, but very slowly and as if she's gasping them.

Most of the time she has a gentle way about her and an angelic smile. But yesterday that changed abruptly.

A few of us were in the common room using headphones to relax with tapes we'd made. All of a sudden we could hear a horrible screaming, which was getting louder as it got closer. Noelle was running down the hall. At first I thought she was running away from someone, but she was heading right for us. Her screaming seemed to be coming straight from her soul, as if all the pain in her entire life could no longer be contained and burst loose in pure fury. She was so out of control I'm not even sure she knew what she was doing, and if it hadn't been for one of the strong nurses who caught hold of her at the last minute, I swear she would have gone after us. It reminded me of my own rage attacks.

The saddest thing about Noelle is so painful that I try not to think about it too much. Sometimes I hear her screaming in the middle of the night. I lie there thinking it's that she realizes, in the endless darkness of her mind, she's alone and lost in a place where no one can reach her, and she is so unbelievably frightened to be who she is.

Chapter 63

FOR THE FIRST TIME in my life, I'm being con-
sistently sensitive to other people and not mostly concerned with myself.

About a week into my stay at the ward, a tall, quiet
guy named William appears in the common area
without a shirt on. The fact that he's partly dressed is
a huge breakthrough. For many years before he came
here, William hadn't been able to wear any clothing.
Just having fabric touch his skin gave him an unbearable feeling. I don't know how he got through life to
this point, but they've been working with him here,
with some obvious success.

Even though the rest of us are in our teens, William appears to be in his thirties and is easily the oldest patient around. He's really intelligent, and his long wild hair makes him look like a mad scientist or some kind of wizard. It seems that most of the people I meet with Tourette's or OCD are unusually smart. Maybe that's just nature's way of compensating, but sometimes I think it's not such a good thing to be so smart and think so much about everything. To be *inside* your mind so much. Maybe it's too easy to get trapped there—like some of us do.

Except on rare occasions, William keeps to himself and stays in his room, which is why I'm surprised to see him in the common area. His obsessions and compulsions are very different from Noelle's, but, like her, he has an awful lot of them. Two of his problems are in direct conflict with each other. He has an extreme phobia of germs. His food has to come from sealed containers, and no one can touch it or be around him when he eats, which is why he never eats with the group. At the same time, another fear makes him deathly afraid to take showers.

William also has a fear of shaving, so his beard is long and scraggly. And he's afraid to lie down on a bed or sit in a chair, so I don't know how he sleeps. Every time I see him, he's standing. He's been standing for so long that his ankles and legs have become terribly swollen.

Germs aren't the only small things that terrify him. One time when he ventured out of his room, he ended up near a girl who was working on an arts-and-crafts project, and she accidentally spilled a bag of glitter. William went totally crazy when he saw it, and he went running off down the hall. I don't know what would have happened if some glitter had actually gotten on him. It's so hard to understand how someone as smart as William can be so irrational about something as harmless as glitter, but that's OCD for you.

"Hey, man," I say as he passes by. He keeps his distance, not because he's antisocial but because he's afraid of any kind of physical contact. He can't touch or be near anyone, even his doctors, so you don't shake hands with William. I can't imagine he's ever high-fived anybody in his entire life. Someone coming up to hug him would probably be his living hell. I wonder how that must have made his parents feel . . . or William himself . . . having to live a life without any physical affection, *ever*.

One of the guys I've become friendliest with has really made me think about what bizarre tricks nature can play on a person's mind. If you ran into my friend

Chester somewhere indoors, you'd think you were with an ordinary, fun-loving guy. He's about fifteen and as all-American-looking as you can get. His interest in rap music isn't unusual either, but his degree of interest is. He always has headphones on, rocking out in the halls, rapping to his favorite songs.

Except with him, it's not just because he likes music. He *needs* to like music, especially songs by the group Linkin Park, whose music he plays over and over again and sings along with. Still, you wouldn't think anything was that different about him.

But something is.

Chester is deathly afraid of daylight. He hates going near the window. And if by accident some sunlight falls on him, he literally freezes in place like a deer caught in the headlights. The one time I saw this happen, he had a look in his eyes as if the world were going to end. Go figure that one out.

Chapter 64

IF YOU HAVE extreme OCD, then Wellington is a very comfortable place to be. Everyone here understands you and could care less if you're different from other people. If I wasn't so homesick I'd have to say I like being here, and I like the kids better than any I've known back in my hometown. They get me, and I get them. They have *empathy*. Most people don't, they really don't.

This is my best week with my clinical psychologist, Mr. Kenneth Roberts. We've been working hard on a number of therapies for almost a month. One is called *cognitive behavioral therapy,* and it is slowly helping me change my everyday thoughts and the way I act.

Wellington's approach to my Tourette's and OCD is completely different from most other approaches. Just like my being sent into the wilderness, this is not the standard treatment for my illnesses. Far from it. It's like a *second* intervention for me.

The main goal now is to deliberately expose myself to my obsessive behaviors, including my Tourette's tics, in order to gain control over them. Before this, my doctors did everything they could to suppress my symptoms.

Every day I focus on my most extreme tics and try to refrain from performing them for longer and longer periods of time. This is part of tic-reversal training.

Right now I can go more than fifteen minutes without doing any unusual movements. There are days when it isn't that good, but little by little I've gotten back some control over my body.

Mr. Roberts thinks that anxiety is at the root of all my other conditions, so he's teaching me a progressive relaxation technique. To help with this, I made a tape that I play in my headphones when I need to calm down. Learning new ways to breathe also helps control my anxiety.

Aside from the treatment, the most important thing about being here is just being here, living in a world where no one is reacting badly to me or judging me.

Chapter 65

SIX WEEKS AFTER arriving at the Wellington clinic, I stand with my suitcase packed. Mr. Roberts rises from his chair in the training room.

It's a hard moment for me because of the feelings I have for him. As my main therapist, Kenneth is one of the best things that has ever happened to me. He seems to instinctively understand what I'm thinking and knows what to say to get me to help myself. I also consider him a friend and a hero to all the people here.

Three of the other patients have assembled in the lounge to say good-bye to me. One college-age girl comes up and hugs me. "You be good," she says with tears in her eyes. "I'm sure you will, Cory."

I know the tears are not only for me. I saw that same look when I bid farewell to my friends at wilderness camp. *You're leaving. And I'm still here.*

"Stay in touch, man!" Chester yells, his headphones still in place.

Chester honestly seems happy for me. Maybe he's glad to see that someone can get enough help to go home. Maybe it gives him hope.

I wish Noelle was around. I'm going to miss her and I know I'll always think about how she's doing. We have been part of a very unusual and close community where we are all safe with one another and the staff. Not like the world I'm about to go back to.

"How are you feeling today?" Mr. Roberts wants to know with his typically serious but gentle and caring manner.

"Really good, I think."

"Can't talk you into staying a little longer, I guess?"

"You can try."

"Hey, that's ... a change."

"But it won't work. I'm outta here."

He shoots me a disappointed but playful look. "You're gonna keep working on that anxiety, right? Do your exercises?"

"Yeah, of course."

"It's easy not to do the exercises when you're back home, but they're important," he says. Right to the bitter end, he's still working with me. You gotta love a guy like that.

From across the room, William's eyes meet mine. He nods, and I return the gesture. We don't need words.

One of the nurses shouts an upbeat good-bye from behind her station window. I take a last look at all the people I'm leaving and feel a wave of guilt that they have to stay. But every one of them is better now than when I met them. And so am I.

When I turn, I see my father at the end of the hall. I can tell that he's been standing there for a while, not wanting to interrupt the ending of this part of my story.

His eyes are glistening. Just like they were at base camp in Wyoming. That's my dad for you.

Chapter 66

I FLY HOME from Wellington and get to stay over for one whole night. Jessie's there, and we connect like we haven't for years. And I can't tell you how good it is to see my mom, my angel.

The next day my mother and father drive me to the Devorough School, a private therapeutic boarding school in western New Hampshire.

As part of a plan I didn't get to vote on, I wasn't allowed to have any contact with my old friends during the brief stopover at my house. I've now been away from home for two and a half months. Going right into another strange new situation is like punishment when I think I should be rewarded. I hate the idea of it. A lot.

My parents have decided to send me right to the Devorough School because it offers me a chance to catch up to my junior-year class before it's too late. This wasn't even a remote possibility before wilderness camp and Wellington. Devorough has an intensive-study program, with more hours per day devoted to lessons than any regular school. Plus, like the other places I've gone to, they are set up to deal with kids who have special problems.

Devorough is in a very rural town and consists of only a few buildings, including a large structure for classrooms, dining, and other activities. Bicycles are the sole mode of transportation allowed other than feet. No friends, no cars, no cell phones, no alcohol, no cigarettes, no life.

We are met by Dr. Marianne Morgan, the founder, in a wheelchair, which reminds me of how far I've come from the days I used to go to school in one. She makes me feel welcome and promises that I will get what I need here. Even though there are many rules that must be followed, the other students love it, she says.

My mother and father are gushing with gratitude for her accepting me. A lot of other schools didn't.

The first group of students I encounter quickly confide that the place is a prison and they totally hate it. Every one of them does. One of the guys I meet right away is a very sketchy, secretive type who seems to command a lot of respect from the other boys. When I try to ask about his past, he doesn't tell me anything, but he's really friendly. He shows me the layout of the school and how to get around some of the rules.

In the next couple of weeks, I undergo intense schooling, but I'm so far behind that I have to stay awake half the night just to catch up. The constant pressure starts to make my tics worse again, which makes studying take even longer.

The relaxation exercises I promised Mr. Roberts I'd keep doing aren't on my mind at all, and even if they were, I wouldn't have time for them anyway.

Because I really do want to catch up to my class back home, I put in an incredible effort, which impresses the staff but takes a toll on me. I'm not getting enough sleep. I'm frantic about falling behind, and I'm getting anxious again. This is the exact opposite of what the people at Wellington wanted to have happen. I'm starting to break down a little.

The pressure isn't helped by a lot of whispering and private discussions going on around my room. I never find out what's going on because the other kids make me leave and no one will tell me anything. I guess I'm too new to be trusted.

I also start having clashes with kids on the lacrosse team when I stupidly brag about how good an athlete I am. I pick a fight with one of the little guys, who easily beats me up. Even after all I've been through, and as good a shape as I'm in, I still haven't got a clue about how to fight.

Every day I'm learning more, and faster, than I ever have before, but the work is still mounting up too fast. In some ways, wilderness camp, with all the snow and ice, was easier than this. I kind of miss the mountains.

Three weeks into my time at Devorough, I feel like I'm going to have a nervous breakdown from the work pressure and lack of sleep. In my mind it's pure torture and punishment. I plead with my parents to let me come home. After a lifetime of their supporting me in so many good ways, this is possibly the worst thing they've ever done and the only mistake in their intervention.

No matter what I say, and it's all the honest truth, they tell me I have to stay until the end of the school year in May.

At night I drift off to sleep thinking about my old friends back home and how I could be with them in a way I never could have before. I feel strong and more in control and want to show them what I'm like now, how I've changed. With my new confidence, I know I can make it in my old high school, maybe even play football again.

I dream of being home, riding my dirt bike, hanging out, sleeping late in my own soft bed.

No one knows it, but I packed my cell phone and charger in a backpack when I came to Devorough. One night I make a call to my old friend Mingo. As usual, he knows what to do, because he's a survivor himself, and he tells me something that hits like a lightning bolt. I've already turned seventeen, so I'm legally old enough to leave Devorough if I want to *without anyone's permission.* No one can stop me, not my parents, not even the police.

My mind starts spinning with the possibilities. Soon, I can think of nothing else but getting away from the school. *It's becoming an obsession.*

The next night, after everyone's asleep, I sneak out a side door and make a break for it. I run like crazy to the two-lane country road that connects Devorough to the nearest town, which I estimate to be ten or fifteen miles away. I feel exhilarated, taking my newfound power and strength and using it to escape from this prison of a school.

Just before midnight, in total spooky darkness, I'm walking on a desolate rural highway.

It's another kind of wilderness, and not nearly as bad as the one I've been to, so I'm okay with it. After an hour, however, I begin to feel that maybe this wasn't such a good idea, because it dawns on me that I escaped without a plan. I left with only the money my parents had given me for school expenses, and I assumed that eventually I would be able to pay someone to drive me back to my hometown. I wasn't thinking, just acting.

Some plan, huh? Talk about compulsive behavior and making bad decisions. I don't even really know how far it is to the next town or how far I've walked, and I'm not dressed for the cold night. After another hour passes, one of the few cars I've seen catches me in its headlights and slows to a crawl. It's a police car.

"Cory Friedman?" the officer asks.

Chapter 67

"YEAH, WHY?" I answer back.

"Been looking for you, son. Get in. I'm taking you back to the school."

I wasn't expecting this. Apparently soon after I escaped, the school did its usual late-night bed check, found me missing, and called the police. It's hard to decide what to do now—then I remember what Mingo told me.

"I don't have to, do I? I'm seventeen," I say very politely, desperately hoping Mingo knew what he was talking about.

"I don't know about that. Even if you are, you have to go back to the school first."

I get in the cruiser, and the policeman returns me to Devorough. The school calls my parents.

When I get on the phone, I refuse my mother's request to stick it out a few more weeks and lash out at both my parents for sending me here. I tell them that I'm demanding my rights and that I'm no longer their dependent son but a legal adult. They don't know how to answer that. It's news to them, like it was to me.

The discussion ends with me hanging up. It turns out that Mingo was right. The police have no choice but to let me leave.

I sign a release that the school needs for their records—this is why I had to go back there. Then the police drive me to the nearest bus station an hour away. It turns out to be such a long distance that I never would have made it on my own.

I don't tell anyone where I'm going. Just far, far away from this prison.

In a few hours I end up at the Port Authority Bus Terminal in New York City and spend the early morning walking the streets. When I'm ready, I take a train to my hometown, where a friend picks me up and drives me home.

My mother and father haven't slept the whole

night. Now that I'm back, they are outraged by my behavior. I understand their position, but I had to do what was right for me. That school sure wasn't. A little while later, I'm safe again in my own bed, and it's the best feeling in the world. I sleep for twenty-two hours straight.

In a few days everything is peaceful again. My parents and I return to Devorough to officially sign me out. We have a final meeting with the school's founder.

"You never should have left us, Cory," she scolds me. I can see how hurt and disappointed she is, but also arrogant, it seems to me. "I don't think you're going to make it out there."

Her words stun me. In my mind this is a cruel and destructive thing to say, but she can't reach me on the inside. After all I've been through, my armor is titanium and a couple of feet thick. I don't argue with her, just thank her for letting me attend. I can't leave the grounds fast enough.

But as we drive away, I'm thinking, *You don't know me. Don't ever count me out. I'm going to make it this time.*

Chapter 68

AFTER DEVOROUGH, there's a sudden shift in focus. Now the job is to try to get me back into my high school to finish junior year. This is almost impossible given all the work I've missed, but not impossible for my mother. She's been on the case, assembling piles of records, making notes, figuring out what we need to do.

We are now on our way to a crucial meeting at school to get me back into classes and discuss any accommodations that they can give me to help me get through the rest of spring semester.

But the moment we walk into the designated

room, our whole idea of what the meeting is about explodes.

The first shock is that this is an actual large conference room, not the customary office space these kinds of meetings take place in, and instead of seeing just the special-ed and guidance counselors needed to take care of my accommodations, we find that the room is loaded with about a dozen people. This stops my mother in her tracks, and she looks as confused as I've seen her in a while.

"Please sit down," someone says sternly, and we take the only two empty seats at the large wooden table.

I don't recognize some of the people here, but there's my history, math, and English teachers; my regular guidance counselor; and a social worker from the special-education department that I met a few times before.

I already have a scary feeling that something is wrong, and I search for the friendly, smiling face of Mrs. Tremaine, my personal caseworker. She's been my best friend in the school administration and has fought for me for years, but for some reason she's not here.

In a moment another woman who's a lot older takes over the meeting. She identifies herself right away. "I'm Emily Hanover. I've been assigned as Cory's new caseworker, *replacing Mrs. Tremaine.*"

For the second time in the first two minutes, my mother and I go into shock. The person who has always been my champion and who I need most in this meeting hasn't even been invited.

Everyone can sense the negative tension. The room is eerily quiet, and I get the feeling that nobody really wants to be here. I know I don't.

When my new caseworker starts again, the world is suddenly turned upside down.

"We wanted to gather everyone familiar with Cory and his history to help you understand why we've come to our decision," she says, looking back and forth between my mother and me.

My mother is stunned by this unexpected announcement.

"What decision? I thought we were here to discuss the accommodations we could have for Cory as he reenters school."

The complete silence that follows tells me how stupid I was to think coming back might be as easy as just asking. And it's a huge surprise that the members of the group have already met on my case and seem to have made up their minds about something big. And bad.

"Basically, we've had to deal with the wisdom of Cory being able to continue in this school year," Mrs.

Hanover says. "It wasn't really a question of how we could help him through the rest of the semester."

I can't help but notice that everything she's saying is in the past tense.

"I don't see any way to avoid the unfortunate fact that Cory simply didn't attend enough of his classes in the first semester to get credit for them," Mrs. Hanover decrees.

It's as if a bomb has been dropped on us. A tidal wave of disappointment rises in my body. My mom looks like she's been punched in the stomach. I want to start screaming but I know this is no time to lose it. Somehow I keep my mouth shut.

"Are you saying that you want Cory to repeat his junior year?" my mother asks, her voice shaking. "Entirely? Starting next fall?"

The magnitude of this thought is still sinking in. *Not going back to school for several months, and then starting over in the same grade?* It's almost impossible to deal with.

It's also almost impossible to understand why none of my "friends" at this meeting are saying anything to defend me, especially my English teacher, who really likes me. She looks as if she's afraid to speak.

As I search from face to face, I see that the one with the most negative look is my history teacher.

This doesn't surprise me, since she never did have much patience with me. I don't think she ever really understood that I can't do all the work all the time or that I can't help being somewhat disruptive in class.

"It's absolutely necessary for Cory to move on," my mother says directly at the new caseworker, confronting her and the whole unexpected premise of the meeting. "I don't know how you can even be thinking about making him repeat junior year."

As she forces herself to continue, I can see her gathering strength. "All of the psychologists agree that Cory needs a new start, and is ready for it. Going backward will only make him revert to where he was when he had to" — she stops short for a moment, then goes on — "when he had to take a leave of absence." She's choosing her words very carefully.

"Look, Mrs. Friedman," my new caseworker says with a sudden pleasantness in her voice. "We're all here because we want what's in Cory's best interest, and we certainly don't want to set him up for failure. As I said, we don't see how Cory can possibly complete the present term since he hasn't really completed the last one."

My mother is speechless.

"He's missed too many days and too much class work. We have thought about this long and hard, and we're in agreement that he doesn't have a chance to succeed in spring semester because he hasn't built the proper foundation for it."

She looks around the room for support from everyone about my terrible crimes of the past, but she doesn't find any. Her voice is still hanging in the air when she sits back in her chair.

"But since I'm the newest person in this," she says, "maybe it would be appropriate to ask for thoughts from those other members of our staff who have worked with Cory . . . just to be fair."

The room goes quiet again as all await her first selection.

"Let's start with his experience in math class."

My math teacher is a little nervous as she begins, and I have no idea what she's going to say. She was always nice to me but not always happy with my performance.

"Cory has shown the potential to be good at mathematics," she starts, "but frankly I don't think at this point he's been in my class enough to grasp a lot of the fundamentals of Algebra I. I tried to keep him up to speed, of course, and when he couldn't attend class, I gave him assignments to do at home, but he didn't turn most of them in."

My mother is about to say something but decides not to.

"Given that, how would you assess his ability to do Algebra II in this next semester?" Mrs. Hanover asks bluntly.

My math teacher hesitates. "It would be very hard for him," she finally admits. "I'd question the wisdom of letting him go to the next level."

I don't think she wanted to say it, but she did.

Mrs. Hanover shifts her attention to my favorite teacher.

"Let's talk about English."

My English teacher seems caught off guard but takes a breath and manages to smile at me kindly. She's obviously uncomfortable.

"Cory has a wonderful mind," she begins. "He's one of my best writers and has a vivid imagination. But... he *has* missed a great many assignments... which isn't to say he still couldn't do well in the spring," she adds as a hopeful afterthought. "English is a little different. His basic skills are in place, but..."

Her words trail off into silence.

"And what's been the experience in history class?" Mrs. Hanover continues.

My heart starts pounding in my chest. My history teacher has been the hardest on me in the whole school. I don't think she's ever liked me. If I have an enemy in the room among the teachers, it's her.

And what she says doesn't surprise me.

"Quite frankly, I don't even have enough work from Cory to say he really has taken first-semester history. He hasn't turned in the majority of his assignments and didn't take his midterm exams. I'm sorry to say that I couldn't possibly pass him on the basis of the work he's completed. He would be cheated of the learning that didn't occur."

What's best for Cory. Question the wisdom of continuing. Cheated of learning.

All the things they're saying are just polite ways of telling us they're not going to help me. *Why don't they just come out and say they don't want to give me a chance, don't even want to listen to our side of things?*

In a while, when Mrs. Hanover finishes with the teachers, she thumbs through a stack of papers in front of her. "There are also, of course, the issues of state educational standards that have to be met. According to Cory's record, he hasn't attended school for enough days to meet the requirement for last term. Technically, the physical education he's missed is enough to set him back by itself."

This seems like a totally random problem to me. The state is very big on gym classes these days, but everyone knows that a lot of the time, nothing much goes on there.

"To be truthful, a good deal of this decision is out of our hands, even though, as I've said, our guiding principle has been to help Cory in any way we can. I think we all agree on that."

Some of the people in the room nod their heads.

Yep, let's help Cory. Let's hold him back.

"So, as you can see, according to the rules, we really have no choice but to require that Cory repeat his junior year. We're sorry, really we are."

Even though this decision has been obvious from the start, I feel a rush of heat. Lucky for me, my mother's hand is around my wrist, grasping it tightly so I can't get up and blow any chance I might have of changing their minds. *If I have any chance at all, which I don't.*

Mom and I exchange glances, and she has to be thinking what I am: *This will destroy everything just when I'm getting better. I have to move forward, not backward. I have to get my life going again, get through high school, and move on.*

"Just give me a chance," she whispers to me calmly, but I can see that she's anything but calm on the inside. I know my mother.

"What it all boils down to," the guidance counselor says when it's his turn to speak, "is that we don't see how Cory can possibly make up what he missed in the fall semester while he's taking on new work in the current term. Up to now there's been some . . . difficulty just keeping up with the regular work—not that he hasn't tried," he adds in a feeble attempt to be kind. "Plus, let's be honest, there's very little time left in the term. It would be a lot to ask of anyone."

"Not for me," I blurt out before I can check myself.

Mom throws me a cautionary look, and I go quiet.

That seems to be the end of the speeches. After a lull, everyone turns to my mother to listen politely to anything she could possibly have to say, to get it over with and then leave. Up until now Mom has let them get more and more negative without arguing, but I know that she won't leave without a fight.

But it takes me off guard when I look at her and see that the unexpected gang-up seems to have been too much, even for her. Her eyes are brimming with tears.

And that's when I can't take it anymore. Suddenly the issue is no longer what's going to happen to me.

"How can you do this to my mother?" I stand up. "Look what you're doing to her. You've made her cry."

Her grip on my wrist tightens, really tightens.

"Don't worry, Mom," I tell her softly. "It isn't worth

it. I'll do anything they want me to. I can do it if I have to."

For a long moment, my mother sits there, collecting herself. I can see she's exhausted, not just from this but from a lifetime of helping me survive an endless number of crises. At last she's come to one that she doesn't have a chance of solving. This is the end of the line, the end of her energy, and I can't blame her for giving up. Too much pain. Too much work. Too many years.

I scan the room again. In the end, not a single teacher has really stepped up to fight the decision that's already been made.

Chapter 69

FOR WHAT SEEMS LIKE A LONG TIME, the group is silent, as if a blanket has been thrown over the room. Then my mother clears her throat and takes a deep breath. It startles me to see that she's undergone a change from just a few minutes earlier.

In place of tears I can see composure, and something more. As I've said before, since the day my head started shaking, Mom has given up her own publishing business, her studies in music, her vacations, and pretty much her life to help me. But one good thing has come out of it. All the time she's invested in me has made her very smart, not only about my situation but also about dealing with doctors, hospitals, and entire school systems. In a way, she's been getting ready for this moment for a long, long time.

When she starts to speak, she's totally in command. And she's my guardian angel all over again.

"Last semester was the hardest Cory has ever had," she begins. "You all know that. His Tourette's and OCD were so out of control he couldn't get to school as much as he'd wanted. He was on a shortened day and was put in the most basic classes just so that he could try to get through junior year.

"There was a time early on when it got too hard for him to walk, and he came to school in a wheelchair just so he wouldn't miss his work. Believe me, that wasn't easy for him. He used to play football and..."

She falters briefly but gathers herself again quickly. My mom just won't quit.

"Cory fought harder than you can imagine to stay in this school, and when that wasn't enough, he took a leave of absence to rehabilitate himself. You know where he went and what he did. Wilderness camp. Sleeping in the snow and freezing cold for a month. And he did it, and came out a survivor. All his counselors agreed on that."

A few heads bob up and down in support. At least they're still listening.

"After that he went to one of the best and hardest OCD hospitals in the world, and he started to turn his life around, a day at a time. It was amazing, and also heroic. And now you're telling him that all this, all his efforts, are just going to be thrown away? *That they don't count for anything?*"

She lets the thought settle in. Her energy and passion are building by the second.

"If you make Cory repeat junior year, you'll be hurting him so much more than helping, and it will cancel out the unbelievable efforts he's made. It will stop his progress cold."

My history teacher starts to lift her hand off the table as if to object, but it's tentative, like she's a student herself, unsure of an answer.

Mom continues without acknowledging her. "But I know you have to go on what he needs to learn. And the rules. So let's talk about the learning he's done that you may not have thought about. Let's talk about that hospital he was in, the Wellington Neurological Center. Do you know that a substantial part of every single day was spent on classroom time, in all subjects? Cory was a star student while he was there. Is that anywhere in your records? It's in *ours*."

She plucks some loose pages from a file and drops them on the table. A couple of the teachers look surprised. This is definitely new information that they're not ready to deal with.

"You all know how innately intelligent Cory is, and about his auditory gift. Whatever he hears in classes, he retains. I know that he's picked up as much knowledge just from sitting in class as most kids do taking notes and doing lessons. Did he miss some things? Yes. Do other kids miss some things?"

She lets the challenge hang in the air. No one interrupts with a rebuttal.

"The Devorough School that Cory went to is an advanced college prep school with a highly accelerated schedule. He was there for only about a month, but I know he learned a lot more than a month's worth of history. And the same goes for chemistry. As a matter of fact, he's already had a good bit of Chemistry II," she adds, training her eyes on Mrs. Hanover, "even when he didn't have the basics of Chemistry I. How? By working seven days a week and staying up late at night studying until he caught up to everyone else. He could do that with algebra, too—in fact, he already started at the Devorough School with some work in Algebra II."

I'm not sure, but I think I can sense a shift of mood

in the room. Everybody, even Mrs. Hanover, is listening hard.

"Did you know that Cory has also done work in areas other students haven't even been exposed to? Last summer, while his friends were playing ball and hanging around, Cory took a seventy-hour course on Web site design. It dealt with designing home pages on the Internet. And this wasn't just any course—it was a course for *college-level students and professionals.* Cory was the youngest one there by far.

"At first they thought he was too young to attend. But in the end, he not only earned their certificate, he was asked to come back to lecture on Internet marketing because of what he knew that they didn't. I understand that he could have been given some credits for that here in high school, but we never asked for them. Now we're asking!"

The guidance counselor perks up at this. He's always encouraged students to learn things outside of school as a way to earn extra credit. This is exactly the kind of stuff he talks about.

"The same goes for the thousands of hours—and I mean thousands—he's spent becoming an expert on the computer at home, studying marketing, taking dozens of courses from experts, publishing articles on Internet marketing, starting five small Internet businesses all by himself. I didn't think to ask for credit for that, but I know credit is given for all kinds of extracurricular learning. I have friends in town who've gotten it for their kids…with letters of recommendation from some of you."

It's amazing to watch and listen to my mother. I never thought about how all the things I've learned on the computer could relate to a high school education, and hearing it all at once, I think it sounds pretty impressive. Even so, my history teacher still isn't making eye contact with my mother and me. She's a tough one.

But Mom has already picked up on her stubbornness. "History? Well, that's not as easy to defend, except I'll tell you this: Cory may not know exactly when the Battle of Waterloo occurred, but his father and I talk about current events all the time. He probably knows as much about what's going on in the world today as any of the other students. And not just the facts but *why* things are happening—the concepts. I guess in this area you could call that homeschooling."

"That's all well and good," the history teacher

interrupts, "but there are specific lessons that have to be completed. Assignments to be done that weren't."

"Yes, I understand that," my mother answers, "and I'm glad you brought it up. As far as all the assignments he's missed, not only in history but in math and English, I want you to see what I found in his backpack at the end of last term."

Mom opens a large manila folder and takes out a stack of papers more than an inch thick.

"These are all homework assignments Cory did on the nights he was able to work. All subjects. It took him a long time to do each of them, and in the end he was exhausted. But no matter how many times I reminded him to turn them in the next day, he usually didn't remember."

"May I?" the history teacher asks suspiciously.

My mother pushes them over to her without comment.

"There are close to sixty assignments here, including fifteen just in history. He did the work; he just didn't get the credit. There was no one at school to remind him to hand them in."

The history teacher inspects the papers and has nothing to say about this latest shocker. Clearly she's starting to lose the basis of her argument.

"But he still didn't take the tests, the midterms," she says anyway.

There is no answer for this. "That's true," my mother admits. Then she continues, "Now, someone mentioned physical education before. So let's talk about eight-mile hikes in deep snow every day for weeks at wilderness camp. What about working on survival skills in twenty-below temperatures? What about losing sixty pounds and quitting smoking and getting incredibly healthy? What have your other students done in physical-education classes this year? How many of them can even come close to Cory's record in gym class?"

With her questions still echoing in the air, she finally takes a moment to catch her breath. We've been in the room for less than an hour, but it's one of the longest meetings of my life.

"Let's be honest," she says, her voice suddenly more relaxed but still serious. "You all know that this isn't about only rules or the number of hours Cory has physically sat in classes. You have enough reason to help him keep going if you want to. That's what it really comes down to. Taking what he has been able to do here so far, thinking about all the amazing things he's achieved out of school, and helping him to build on them, helping him to keep going, like you always have before. You've always been on his side. Most of you have been wonderful to him. Why turn your backs on him now?"

Nearing the end of her talk, my mom looks at me tenderly. Her face is glowing. She looks so beautiful I can't begin to describe it.

"This is one amazing kid," she says to the room. "Don't ever give up on him. He'll always surprise you and come through for you."

After a long silence, there's another voice in the room. It's that of my English teacher, speaking her true thoughts for the first time.

"Cory is my best student," she starts quietly, then her voice rises. "By far my best. His ideas get the other students excited to learn."

The room is quiet again. Outside in the hallway, there are kids rushing somewhere. The English teacher's compliment feels great, but one voice is probably not enough. If the group is beginning to change its mind, it's impossible to tell.

The caseworker turns to me and asks if there's anything I want to say. Before I can respond, the history teacher demands to know how I can possibly do all the work now when I couldn't get it done before. Amazingly, she isn't giving up. After what my mother has told her, I really don't know what else I can say, so I just tell them all how I feel.

"Things have always been harder for me," I say simply. "But that's never stopped me, and it never will."

Chapter 70

IT SEEMED TO HAPPEN TO ME when I wasn't even aware of it. Or maybe it occurred over a few days, or even weeks. You would think that if I'd known the *exact* moment of anything that's ever happened in my life, it would be this.

It's the last period of the school day toward the end of my junior year, and I'm doing pretty well. I still can't believe that I sat through all eight periods again today. One reason may be that I'm not on most of the drugs that used to make me feel so out of it.

In history class the Civil War is coming alive for me. It's as if I'm living back in that time, and the

313

teacher likes my answers. The history teacher likes my answers! *The history teacher—how about that!* As usual, my hand has been shooting up in the air a lot, but only with questions and answers, not with my usual middle-finger salute.

When the period ends, I leave the room feeling that something important has changed, but I'm not sure what. I have an unusual sense of well-being, as if the electric current that usually races around my body has suddenly been turned way down, as though it's on a dimmer.

At the exit I push open the door and step into bright sunshine. The puffy clouds in the sky are so interesting that I stop for a while to study them.

The clouds are lit from behind by the sun, which is highlighting their wispy edges and making them glow as if a great artist has painted them. There was a sky something like this in the mountains of Wyoming not so long ago.

I take a few more moments to watch the sky. There's no hurry. I feel like I have all the time in the world.

Finally I walk toward the end of the parking lot, where my car is parked. On the way I pass the handicapped spots that I was told I could use for my dirt bike and that I always refused.

Walking to my car, I realize that I have an unusual amount of energy and concentration, plus I'm light on my feet.

Normally at this time of day I'd be totally exhausted and on edge, ready to go home and rest from my classes. My new feelings puzzle me. I play back the day in my mind and am happy to recall that none of my classes turned out to be a problem.

The realization comes over me, not like a bolt of lightning, as people say, but like a calm breeze that creeps into my mind and spreads a peaceful blanket of serenity.

I'm not ticcing. I'm not ticcing at all.

Chapter 71

THE THOUGHT IS SO MIRACULOUS, so *impossible,* that I automatically dismiss it. I can't actually remember if it's been this way all day, but I feel weak at the knees from the possibility that it might be true. I'm just standing there as other kids are passing by and noticing me, a few saying hello.

Out of habit I wait for familiar urges to come back—the need to contort my face, to hop or lurch forward, to dip to one side or bend at the waist. I count the seconds until my arm will undoubtedly shoot out three times in front of me to punch the air, or my neck will tilt up to the sky.

And what's happening is *nothing*.

A different kind of panicky feeling begins to take hold of me, the fear that this is going to end any second.

I need to divert myself from thinking about ticcing because that's what always brings it on.

In a little while, when the movements still aren't happening, I test them by challenging myself to tic. Deliberately I jerk my hand in front of my chest, but I have no compulsion to complete the ritual with the usual two more thrusts.

I still think this is all a bizarre mistake, a miscalculation my brain has made that will soon be corrected.

Or maybe I'm dreaming the whole thing. I've dreamed it so many times before, but this seems real. Even if it's crazy or is a temporary mistake or only lasts a short time, at least I know that it's possible.

I travel the rest of the way to my car without a single hop and with a sense of wonder.

On the ten-minute drive home, my foot is steady on the gas pedal and I don't have the involuntary stiffening of my leg that makes me speed up. I don't jerk the wheel to the right or left, not even once. I don't jack up the volume on the radio before turning it on.

When my mother greets me at the door, I'm too

afraid to tell her what's going on. Raising her hopes only to have them crushed again would be an unbearably unkind act, and it's still too early to risk it.

Jessie is in the living room, and she flashes me a gentle smile. As I've gotten better, we've gotten closer again. I know she's proud of how far I've come. As a senior, Jessie applied to six colleges and got accepted to five of them. She's going after the degree in special ed that she's always wanted. The thought of not having her around saddens me, but I have something else to think about today.

An hour later, the tics still haven't returned, and I have to at least allow for the possibility that something has really changed.

By eight o'clock I've finished my homework in record time and I'm sitting at the computer, playing with some new ideas for an Internet marketing business.

My hands are unbelievably steady on the keys, and I feel no need to pound the table after every few words like I used to. My eyes and mouth are still.

This really is happening, isn't it?

The doctors have said that Tourette's symptoms improve over time for some people, but not all. Have I turned out to be one of the lucky ones?

If my parents have noticed a change, they aren't saying anything, probably for the same reason I'm not. They're conditioned not to mention my physical habits unless I do, but I know they're always watching out of the corner of their eyes, praying to see exactly what's happening now. *Nothing at all.*

Later, I head for bed in a state of total wonder but also apprehension. On the way up the stairs, I catch my mother looking at me.

"I know," I tell her. "Don't say anything."

Chapter 72

THE NEXT MORNING I lie in bed, afraid to get up and see that I'm the same person I always was.

I can't tell yet if anything's changed because the best time for me is usually when I first wake up. I know I should be incredibly excited at the prospect of a day of being like everyone else, but excitement is always my enemy, and the fear that today I will return to the *old me* is almost paralyzing. I honestly don't know if I could take the fall.

Still, I stand up, and I test myself.

Leaving my room for the shower, I remember that

doorways can make me do a compulsive little triple shuffle step before I can pass through.

This time I sail through without anything happening.

Soon my body is enveloped in hot water and steam, and I'm sinking into a deep state of relaxation. I look down at the busted floor tiles...and wonder if I'm really done breaking them.

I get to the kitchen smoothly, letting the idea of a miracle sink in. The quiet feeling is with me again today, as though I'm under anesthesia but have remained awake and alert.

I want to shout my sudden happiness at the top of my lungs, to wake the world and say, *Look at me,* but I still don't dare to assume that this is real.

I go to school feeling good but worried that this is where it will end. But even the stress of another day of sitting in the confined space of my classrooms isn't changing me back. Today is starting like yesterday ended, completely calm.

My classes are easier than they've ever been, and I can't stop myself from participating. Maybe I'm participating too much; one of my teachers asks me to give the other students a chance to share with the class. Fair enough. I can do that.

In between periods I walk down the halls like everyone else. It's amazing to me what a luxury, what a gift, normal walking is. I'm not sure, but I think the kids are looking at me differently. They're not avoiding my eyes like they do when I stumble or make a noise. A few of them greet me warmly as I pass by. I'm fascinated by the thought that today might be the first day I don't get any strange looks or hear muffled laughter after I leave a hallway or room.

After school I walk the streets of my hometown as if for the very first time. In a way, it is.

The early-spring breeze feels good on my skin as I come to the pizza place where a lot of kids from the high school hang out. This is the same restaurant where a customer once called the police because she thought I was having seizures.

I talk to some kids I know—without twitching. I'm in full control. I have a new urge now, but it's a good one—to be with everyone I've ever known and let them see me as I suddenly am. Now they can judge me for what I say and do, not how I move.

Chapter 73

LATER THAT NIGHT, when my family's asleep, an idea takes shape that's been rumbling around in my mind for hours, or maybe years. I sneak out of bed and hurry down the hallway stairs without making a sound.

I gently pry open the front door and leave the house.

The night is warm as I step up to my dirt bike and straddle the seat. I put it in neutral and walk the heavy machine out to the end of the driveway so the engine won't wake anyone in our house.

Once I'm out on the street, the bike comes alive

under me, and when I start moving, I look back at my home, my eyes filling with tears. For more than a decade, this has been my refuge and my prison. Most of the time I've been afraid to leave. But not tonight.

The engine sputters once when I rev it and shift into higher gear. Then it smooths to a purr. In a way, this is like what's just happened to me. *Sputtering, missing, then running smooth.*

For the next few hours, I ride the streets of our town in darkness and anonymity, my bike and I in perfect harmony for the first time. The road, the whole world, is empty. Yet for me it's never been so full of promise and hope.

I shift into third gear, give it the gas, and take off, laughing.

I am alive.

I am free.

I am flying with the wind.

I am me.

A Father's Epilogue

IN JANUARY 2002, my son lay in the darkened basement of our house in a downward spiral of depression, alcohol addiction, and hopelessness, and he made the decision to change. *He did it himself.* Roughly three months later, he began to reclaim his life with astonishing new strength and an irrepressible determination to beat the overwhelming odds against him.

It had taken years of debilitating neurological problems to bring Cory close to his breaking point. He suffered from one of the most complex cases of

OCD, Tourette's syndrome, and anxiety disorder his doctors had ever seen. Even though our family lived through each and every moment of his resurrection, we could hardly believe that his recovery had happened. It was a miracle.

When the members of the high school administration decided to allow Cory to complete his junior year, they laid out a daunting number of requirements. In addition to having to take the new midterms, he had to make up some past midterm exams, including the history test, on which he received an A. Several weeks later, he took the final history exam for the fall semester, which he also aced. These accomplishments were achieved in major part by his studying hundreds of three-by-five note cards prepared and gone over time and again by his mother. Maybe a hundred hours' worth.

Cory's English teacher waived all the past smaller assignments and asked only for the junior-year formal paper. He completed this task as well, a phenomenal essay on Walt Whitman for which he also got an A.

After that spectacular show of what he could do, and because most of the teachers and administrators really were on his side, they had no choice but to pass him on to the next semester.

After that, Cory had only one surprising request, a very revealing one: that he be allowed to take a few advanced courses instead of just basic ones. He had won his chance to prove himself, and that's what he set out to do.

During the remainder of that school year, teachers and students alike were astonished to see what the boy who once came to only a few basic-level classes a day—and for a while in a wheelchair—was capable of.

In the little time left in the spring term, Cory completed practically *two* terms at once without missing a single day. In the end he satisfied all of the school's criteria, passed every exam, and earned an A average. His teachers voted him the most-improved student in a high school of seven hundred.

In his senior year, Cory's progress continued just as dramatically.

That spring his name was called at the graduation ceremony on the same field where he'd once thrilled the crowd with his football play. On that fateful day the tears flowed freely, and not just from our family.

The main credit, of course, goes to Cory himself and his irrepressible spirit; also to one very special therapist who never left us even after she moved away; and to a few wonderful champions he had in our school system.

It also helped, we believe, that Cory was always told—and therefore always assumed—there was nothing in life he couldn't accomplish, no matter what the obstacles.

Cory's mother, his true angel, never faltered in that arena. Not once did I ever see my wife, Sophia, let up under pressure or give in to despair. She has always been, and remains, an endlessly loving, unselfish, and giving human being with no other agenda than her family's well-being. I am certain beyond a doubt that her strength has become Cory's, not to mention mine.

During his senior year, Cory applied to a number of colleges with the rest of his classmates. His résumé was unlike any of theirs, however. To offset gaps in his formal education caused by absences, he created a unique portfolio that presented an unusual record of achievements outside the classroom. This included his experience on the computer, his place of refuge during years of isolation from friends.

One day in April 2003, a little more than a year after he walked out of the wilderness camp, Cory opened a letter that informed him that, against all odds, he'd been accepted into the School of Information Studies at Syracuse University. This was a moment for Cory and the rest of our family that was simply impossible to describe.

At Syracuse, Cory's professors were so impressed with his computer marketing knowledge that he was offered his own office in the Information Studies School, one of only six, and he was even asked to lecture at one of their classes. He became the lead singer in a band and performed in front of hundreds of students, once receiving a cheering ovation from the same basketball team that had won a national championship.

As of this writing, some of Cory's physical symptoms still return, but they are nowhere near as severe as they used to be. He is on very little medicine, and he's not taking anything that coincided with a worsening of his symptoms in the past. Our family is convinced that his most extreme symptoms were caused by medications prescribed in good faith but with unhappy results, almost without exception. Cory's battle to control OCD has been more successful, as he brings to bear his hard-won coping skills from Wellington. His optimism knows no bounds.

A complete cure for Tourette's remains elusive. Within the past few years, however, a young man with a vastly more extreme movement disorder had a pioneering operation at the Cleveland Clinic. From reports we've heard, it stopped all of his symptoms instantly.

Since then a number of operations involving Tourette's patients have been performed at this clinic and at other hospitals around the world. Exact information on their success is difficult to obtain, as official clearance is still pending, but we have heard that the results are promising, and there will be more trials.

Today, Cory is deeply involved in Internet marketing and has created a number of fledgling businesses of his own. He frequently makes trips to New York City to sing at karaoke clubs and is a lead singer in a really good band in New Jersey that's just formed. As always, no obstacle seems too great for him.

Over the thirteen long, hard years that this story covers, Cory had dreams that some people would consider modest. He wanted to go to school, play sports, have friends, and be treated with respect. These are things a normal childhood provides, but they were not often Cory's to enjoy. Yet despite his complex problems and many cruel setbacks, he always clung to the belief that he would survive his travails and achieve a happier life. And over time, this belief has only strengthened.

He has been to the bottom of the abyss, but he has been to the top of the mountain as well.

Appendix

New Zoloft { 1 pill
3½ Risperdol

I never did have the courage to
take Cory off all Risperdol. He
has been on 3-4 mg since
the beginning of school year.
Academically, with lots of support
(continuous contact w. school ie:
writing homework down, typing his
work and in-class support w.
math, reading & lang. arts) he has
done fairly well - A's & B's.

Socially - We are at an all-time
low! No one has called him
for months!!

Tics - has suffered with
numerous tics, particularly
internal stomach tics and
shoulder tic. These have
produced pain!

Vocal bantering - terrible. always
has need to provoke!!!

*Sample of extensive medical records detailing medicines,
side effects, and behavior from September 29, 1999,
through January 4, 2000.*

Depakote ⎫ vocal tic became quite
Rispeidal ⎬ severe. Only change
Ativan ⎭ is depakote

On Depakote – ▓▓▓▓▓▓▓▓▓

Big Question: Did Depakote worsen
vocal tic

Side effect: (couldn't sleep)

I complained so much, we took him
off. Still bad weekend

Cony is becoming frantic

★ Remmon) – started tues.
antidepresant that's sedating

336

Cory asked

Am I in hell?

What am I suppose to do next?
Why don't I know?

What do I do every day?

Why don't I know that I should
go on the computer?

I have a bad feeling that
makes me feel nothing
is going to go is right

I can never relax like other people

I get bad feelings every day

When I was riding in car with
Dad, every time he talked I
knew I was going to
hear a loud noise —
and I did — Everything
gets ruined

337

Cory had a severe tic day & night (Sat. ████████)

meds

Did adding 12½ mgs. of zoloft do this?

If I give up too quickly on zoloft, I'll never know whether antidepressants can help her obsessional thoughts

* Cory told me Friday " I realize, now, that I can make my tics worse. I think about them, worry, and they get worse."

Buspar - 15 mg 3x day
Risperdal 1½ mg - bedtime
→ Tenex - 1½ pills - (divided AM + PM)
Atavan - 5 pills (AM, After-bed)
→ * Celexa - 20 mg (AM)

Most Prominent Tic - leg shuffle -
quite severe - esp. going in +
out of doors

Compulsions - touch people (r. annoying
to friends)

Changes

→ Zoloft - Didn't work out - teachers
complained he was o. agitated

* Celexa - 1st antidepressant he
is tolerating. Seems calmer,
able to watch some TV
(couldn't before)

→

Cory went to school in wheelchair —
leg tic too severe

Raising Alexa? Did increase make
tic worse? On going back to
school.

I want to stay course to see.

Improvement

V. marked change — able
to watch TV & movies).
Hasn't for years. Must be
Alexa.

Longer fuse

Checked ▮ 1am – 100/60

Horrendous night – Tics have been keeping him from sleeping. Cory asked to go to hospital for injection to "put him to sleep"

We are at a frightening point – Cory is at his worst and we seem to have run out of drugs.

Orap
Telradrazine

Risperdal
Zyprexia
Ativan
✓ Buspar
✓ Tenex
✓ Clonidine
Zoloft
Prozac
Celexa
Neurontin
Depakote

Aricept
Remeron

!
.

hopefully, aricept, if it exacerbate things will leave his system today

1½ Risp
Buspar   15 3x day
Ativan   4-6 per day
Tenex—   ½ am   1½ pm
Clexa   ↓ 1 pill

Despite the fact that Comp
attention to TV has improved,
he's leg tic is horrendous — got
him out of wheelchair, but I
honestly don't know how he is
doing it. He shuffles backwards
violently. Has fallen a few times
I lowered Clexa in last few
days from 1¾ to 1

Restless
hot   ⎧ v. pronounced when
Complaining of tics   ⎨ his mind is not
                                 ⎬ engaged — sitting
                                 ⎩ + doing nothing

Unfortunately, besides computer, there

2 mg Risperdal
Ativan (as per needed, plus 2 2mg at
    bedtime)

Seizing whole body
leg tic   } very bad slope
assorted small tics

Again - We took a trip, this time
    to Florida

Except for new "seizing" tic, we have
    a basic repeat of last year:

        tics so bad, he's now not able
        to be at school.

neurologist ████████ wants to rule
        out seizures. EEG 4/4/10

Traditional Allergist - next week

            →

343

Medicines Prescribed for Various Symptoms and Taken over a Thirteen-Year Period

Neuroleptic/ Antipsychotic	Antidepressants	Blood Pressure/Agitation
Geodon	Anafranil	clonidine
Haldol	Celexa	Tenex
Orap	Effexor	
Risperdal	fluvoxamine	*Muscle Relaxer*
Seroquel	Paxil	baclofen
tetrabenazine	Remeron	
Zyprexa	trazodone	
	Wellbutrin	
	Zoloft	

Antidyskinetic	ADHD	Antinausea
Cogentin	Ritalin	Zofran

Anxiety/ Sedation	Anticonvulsants/ Mood Stabilizers	Beta-Blocker
Ativan (lorazepam)	Aricept	Inderal (propranolol)
Benadryl	Depakote	
BuSpar	Lamictal	
Klonopin	Neurontin	
Valium	nicotine patch	
Xanax	Tegretol	
	Topamax	

Vitamins and Minerals

*(All taken daily for approximately six weeks,
in addition to prescription medicines)*

beta-carotene	selenium
calcium	vitamin B_1
fish oil	vitamin B_2
glutathione	vitamin B_3
grape seed extract	vitamin B_6
inositol	vitamin B_{12}
lecithin	vitamin C
magnesium	vitamin E
pantothenic acid	zinc
para-aminobenzoic acid (PABA)	

About the Authors

JAMES PATTERSON published his first thriller in 1976 and since then has become one of the best-known and bestselling writers of all time, with more than 140 million copies of his books sold worldwide. He is the author of the two most popular detective series of the past decade, featuring Alex Cross and the Women's Murder Club, and he has written numerous other #1 bestsellers. He has won an Edgar Award—the mystery world's highest honor—and his novels *Kiss the Girls* and *Along Came a Spider* were made into feature films starring Morgan Freeman. His charity, the James Patterson PageTurner Awards, has given hundreds of thousands of dollars to individuals and groups that promote the excitement of books and reading. He lives in Florida.

HAL FRIEDMAN has published five works of fiction. He lives with his wife, Sophia, at the edge of a forest in northern New Jersey.

THE NOVELS OF JAMES PATTERSON

Featuring Alex Cross

Double Cross
Cross
Mary, Mary
London Bridges
The Big Bad Wolf
Four Blind Mice
Violets Are Blue
Roses Are Red
Pop Goes the Weasel
Cat & Mouse
Jack & Jill
Kiss the Girls
Along Came a Spider

The Women's Murder Club

7th Heaven (coauthor Maxine Paetro)
The 6th Target (Maxine Paetro)
The 5th Horseman (Maxine Paetro)
4th of July (Maxine Paetro)
3rd Degree (Andrew Gross)
2nd Chance (Andrew Gross)
1st to Die

The James Patterson Pageturners

The Dangerous Days of Daniel X
*The Final Warning: A Maximum Ride
Novel*
*Maximum Ride: Saving the World and
Other Extreme Sports*
Maximum Ride: School's Out — Forever
Maximum Ride: The Angel Experiment

Other Books

Against Medical Advice: A True Story
(coauthor Hal Friedman)
Sail (Howard Roughan)
Sundays at Tiffany's
You've Been Warned (Howard
Roughan)
The Quickie (Michael Ledwidge)
Step on a Crack (Michael Ledwidge)
Judge & Jury (Andrew Gross)
Beach Road (Peter de Jonge)
Lifeguard (Andrew Gross)
Honeymoon (Howard Roughan)
SantaKid
Sam's Letters to Jennifer
The Lake House

The Jester (Andrew Gross)
The Beach House (Peter de Jonge)
Suzanne's Diary for Nicholas
Cradle and All
When the Wind Blows
Miracle on the 17th Green (Peter de
   Jonge)
Hide & Seek
The Midnight Club
Black Friday (originally published as
   Black Market)
See How They Run (originally
   published as *The Jericho
   Commandment*)
Season of the Machete
The Thomas Berryman Number

For previews of upcoming books by James Patterson
and more information about the author,
visit www.JamesPatterson.com.